MADAME MÈRE

BY THE SAME AUTHOR
Napoleon's St. Helena
Napoleon Surrenders
Napoleon's Last Journey

MADAME MÈRE

Napoleon's Mother

❈   ❈   ❈

Gilbert Martineau

*Translated from the French
by Frances Partridge*

JOHN MURRAY

© Gilbert Martineau 1978
This translation
© John Murray (Publishers) Ltd 1978

All rights reserved. No part of this publication
may be reproduced, stored in a retrieval system or
transmitted, in any form or by any means,
electronic, mechanical, photocopying, recording or
otherwise, without the prior permission of
John Murray (Publishers) Ltd
50 Albemarle Street, London W1X 4BD

Printed in Great Britain by
Cox & Wyman Ltd, London, Fakenham and Reading
0 7195 3459 3

To
RAINER OF HESSE
This book is inscribed by his
FRIEND

It is to my mother, it is to her good principles that I owe my success and any good there is in me.
      NAPOLEON

Her soul was worthy of Plutarch, that is to say the exact opposite of that of an ordinary princess.
      STENDHAL

My son was overthrown, he died miserably very far from me; my other children are outlaws; I watch them die, one after another. I am old, forsaken, without glory or honours. Yet I would not change my fate for that of the first queen in the world.
      MADAME MÈRE

I believe that saintly woman to be worthy of the veneration of all earthly princes.
      PIUS VIII

What a beautiful character! Where in Europe is there a queen with such an exalted moral nature?
      STENDHAL

I am more than an empress: I am the mother of the great Napoleon.
      MADAME MÈRE

Madame Mère has won the esteem of the people, the love of her friends and the respect of all.
      DUKE OF HAMILTON, 1828

Contents

1	'Beautiful as a Goddess'	1
2	'The Widow Buonaparte'	19
3	'Madame Letizia Buonaparte, seamstress'	32
4	'The Mother of Bonaparte'	41
5	'Her Imperial Highness, Madame, mother of His Majesty the Emperor'	62
6	'The Corsican Niobe'	122
7	'The Mother of all Sorrows'	142
8	'Open, eternal gates!'	168
	Select Bibliography	189
	Index	191

Illustrations

The House of the Bonaparte, Napoleon's birth place, at Ajaccio. From a painting by A. Daligé de Fontenay in the Musée de Malmaison. *Photo: Laverton-Rueil*   *f.p.* 6

Charles Bonaparte from an engraving by Delpech. *Photo: Bibliothèque Nationale*, Paris   7

Letizia Bonaparte, a bust by Chaudet. *Photo: Bibliothèque Nationale*, Paris   7

Bonaparte in 1797 from a watercolour by Cassia painted at Verona, in the Napoleon Museum, Arenenberg. *Photo: Willy Müller*   22

Bonaparte, Lieutenant of Artillery, from an engraving by T. Johnson after a painting by Jean-Baptiste Greuze. *Copyright: Mansell Collection, London*   22

Madame Mère and bust of Napoleon, at the Musée de Malmaison. *Photo: Laverton-Rueil*   23

Joseph Bonaparte, King of Spain, 1768–1844*   54

Napoleon, by Gérard, in the Musée Cade, Chantilly. *Copyright: Mansell Collection, London*   54

Lucien Bonaparte, Prince of Canino, 1775–1840*   54

Elisa Bacciochi, Princess de Lucques et de Piombino, 1777–1820*   54

Louis Bonaparte, King of Holland, 1778–1846*   55

Pauline Borghese, Duchesse de Gustalla, 1780–1825, from a portrait by Robert Lefèvre. *Crown Copyright: Wellington Museum, London*   55

Illustrations

Caroline Murat, Queen of Naples, 1782–1839*	55
Jerome Bonaparte, King of Westphalia, 1784–1860	55
Madame Mère from a portrait by Robert Lefèvre in the Museo Napoleonico, Rome. *Archivio Fotografico of the Museo di Roma*	70
One of Madame Mère's court dresses in the Museo Napoleonico, Rome. *Archivio Fotografico of the Museo di Roma*	70
Bust of Madame Mère by Canova in the Museo Napoleonico, Rome. *Archivio Fotografico of the Museo di Roma*	71
Bust of Madame Mère by Tricornia and Franzoni in the Musèe de Malmaison. *Photo: Laverton-Rueil*	118
Cardinal Fesch by Canova in the Ajaccio Museum. *Photo: A. Moretti*	118
Madame Mère by F. J. J. Sieurac in the Museo Napoleonico, Rome. *Photo: Archivio Fotografico of the Museo di Roma*	119
Letizia Ramolino-Bonaparte by an unknown artist in the collection of Count Ramolino de Coll'Alto	134
Madame Mère in her old age, drawn by her grand-daughter Charlotte. From a lithograph in the Museo Napoleonico, Rome	135
Madame Mère's death mask, after a cameo by Coquille. *Photo: Bibliothèque Nationale, Paris*	135

*Reproduced from a book of lithographs of the collection of Mr Alfred D. Pardee

I
'Beautiful as a Goddess'

The marriage of Letizia Ramolino, thirteen- or fourteen-year-old niece of the canon of Ajaccio cathedral, to Carlo Buonaparte, nephew of the archdeacon, was doubtless a typical Corsican ceremony.* Perhaps the young girl was escorted to meet her bridegroom by *Mugliaccheri*, or pages of honour; probably she conformed to custom – she was highly superstitious – by washing her hands in a stream on the way, to purify herself; probably, too, her women friends showered her with rice, corn, sweets and small coins to ensure her future happiness and prosperity. On arrival at the Casa Buonaparte she must certainly have been given the symbolic flower representing the key to the conjugal home. And a large crowd was present at the ceremony on June 2, 1764, in that lovely cathedral built in the Venetian style by the architect of one of the popes. What could be more natural? These two well-known and respected families had innumerable relations.

'My mother was attended by fifty first cousins at her wedding, fine handsome men,' Napoleon liked to recall.

The three branches of the Buonaparte family had been

---

* The exact date of Letizia's birth is not known for certain, as the archives of the Town Hall of Ajaccio were destroyed during the Revolution; but if her own statements are to be trusted ('I was married at the age of thirteen . . . I was a widow at thirty-three.'), she must have been born about 1751. Until 1759, the Buonapartes spelled their name in the Corsican style, 'Bonaparte'. At that date they were recognised by the patrician branch in Tuscany and began signing themselves 'Buonaparte', in the Italian style.

established at Bologna, Treviso and Florence ever since the ninth century, and included among their numbers counts, ambassadors, municipal officials and priors. The Ajaccio branch had descended through eleven generations from Francisco Buonaparte who came to Corsica in 1490; they were entitled to bear arms ('gules with three silver cotises and two stars, each with six rays of the same') and were all well-known people. The Ramolinos, for their part, were related to the Counts of Coll'Alto, a noble Lombard family, and had settled in the island two centuries earlier, under the protection of the Genoese Republic; they were mostly soldiers or officials.

Carlo Buonaparte, a tall handsome young man, always elegantly dressed but with a rather weak face, had been orphaned at the age of fourteen and brought up ever since by his uncle the Archdeacon Lucien, a forceful character, who had watched over the first steps of the future head of the family carefully and parsimoniously. Carlo was educated at Ajaccio and Corte, then at Pisa, and was destined for the bar like his father, who had been a member of the Council of Ancients of Ajaccio. His fortune was small, consisting mainly of the income from two vineyards, some meadows and two floors in the Casa Buonaparte. Letizia, 'beautiful as a goddess', was the daughter of an Inspector of the Department of Civil Engineering and of an aristocratic girl from Sartène called Angela-Maria di Pietra-Santa, but nothing is known about her childhood.* Her dowry consisted of a few acres of land, a kiln with rooms adjoining, another apartment in Ajaccio and some vineyards, the whole valued at about 7000 *livres*. It wasn't a gold-mine, and appearances had to be kept up, but the two young people could have lived according to their station, and happily too, if their temperaments had not been so completely opposed (Carlo was an unbeliever and his wife devout; he was a spend-

---

* Only that she was lovely to look at, that they called her 'the little marvel' in Ajaccio, and that some curates who were probably not indifferent to her charms said that 'her beauty made more converts than a hermit did by his saintliness'. How gallantly Corsicans expressed these things!

thrift, she parsimonious), and above all if politics had not been spreading discord throughout the island and its clans.

The Genoese said it was the Corsicans' fault, and the Corsicans accused the Genoese administration. Since an occupying power is never popular, it was easy to propagate the belief that the island was being suffocated by a Serene Republic in full decline. The islanders had rebelled in 1734, taking as their leader Giacinto Paoli, a native of Morosaglia, and nominating him commander-in-chief and primate of a kingdom of which the Virgin Mary had been appointed Queen. After an absurd interlude – the ephemeral reign of King Theodore I, a minor German nobleman and adventurer supported by the British, with Giacinto Paoli as Prime Minister – the Corsicans elected Giacinto's son, Pasquale Paoli as commander-in-chief. He was a good patriot who had served in Naples, and returned to his native land full of dreams of justice à la Jean-Jacques Rousseau and who, believing the island to be more advanced politically than it actually was, granted it a Council, a parliament in the English style and even a Constitution. This was fast and furious going, seeing that Genoa still held the supreme authority legally, if in no other manner.

In the same year as the marriage the Serene Republic, tired of these successive rebellions, offered Corsica to France outright, in payment of some pressing debts, and Louis XV's forces occupied Ajaccio, Bastia, Calvi, Saint-Florent and Algajola: this did not yet amount to complete cession, but would today be diplomatically and discreetly termed 'offering facilities' to a friendly power which was anxious to avoid England laying hands on this part of the Mediterranean.

That generous prince, the King of France, unsuccessfully proposed that Paoli should command the Royal Corsican regiment, with the title of King of Corsica 'under the sovereignty and guarantee of France'. But once installed at Corte, the stubborn fellow would hear of nothing short of an independent Corsica, or having allegiance to England alone. Such audacity towards a powerful 'protector', who was already installed, was highly attractive to the young, and Carlo Buonaparte, who was still at the University and living at Corte, was one of those who hurried to put themselves forward and obtain posts. Appointed secretary to the great man and then to the Council – it was even said that he drew up official proclamations and wrote his chief's speeches – he sent for his young wife to the capital of the resistance movement, and Letizia's great adventure began.

She had lost one child in 1765 and another in 1767, but on January 7, 1768, she gave birth to Joseph, a fine boy who survived, to the great delight of his young father. This simple family happiness was of short duration, for in May came the shattering news that Genoa had finally and definitely ceded Corsica to France, and Paoli's Council declared war on Paris, an act of folly whose implications were disguised by loud cries of 'Death rather than slavery!' in the streets of the old mountain town. This mood of exaltation was kept going by a victory over the French troops on October 8, but then . . . in spite of his first success, the fair-haired, blue-eyed Corsican Paoli found his position untenable. He was a good statesman – no doubt about that; he had organised the executive, legislative and judiciary departments, established schools and even a University (the one attended by Carlo Buonaparte), raised a militia and encouraged agriculture. His enemies called him the 'general of the spuds' – he had drained marshes, opened the port of Calvi and even minted money. After a ten years' struggle, the Genoese gave up and the French were beaten, but the days of Corsican independence were numbered and the weakest went to the wall when Versailles put their forces under the command of the Comte de Vaux, an experienced general, who did not stint reinforcements, either as to number or quality, launching along the rough mountain roads those famous *Gribeauval* guns, which some years later helped Napoleon win his battles. Common sense would have dictated negotiation, but pride spurred on resistance, and it was pride – a form of heroism – that carried the day.

On May 9, 1769, after a pitched battle on the banks of the river

'Beautiful as a Goddess'

Golo, Paoli was left without an army, and sailed for England. His supporters fled in disorder, with their wives and children, among them a young woman of nineteen, six months pregnant, supported by her husband – Letizia Buonaparte. Riding on horseback over rocky tracks, crossing streams transformed into torrents by the melting snows, sleeping in caves, feeding on bread, milk and chestnuts, Carlo and his wife at last reached Ajaccio, where they at once realised the extent of the catastrophe: the French held Corte, where the members of a general Council were voting to swear fidelity to Louis XV. The annexation of Corsica only cost the King of France eleven officers and eighty soldiers killed in battle.

Nevertheless, on August 15 Ajaccio celebrated the festival of her patron saint the Virgin, and Archdeacon Lucien officiated. Letizia was praying ardently, for she was deeply and sincerely religious, when she had to leave the church in haste because of the movements within her of the child she was expecting, and had been carrying over the battlefields. She hurried back to the Casa Buonaparte, where she was seized by pangs, collapsed on a sofa covered in green cloth, and gave birth to a rather puny boy with an enormous head.* It was twelve o'clock and all the bells were ringing in honour of the mother of God.

The child was christened Napoleon – *Nabulione* in the Corsican patois and *Nabulio* to the family – in memory of an uncle of his father's, who had died several months earlier fighting the French – those same French whom Carlo was soon to seek out as daily companions with tranquil philosophy.†

* Legend embellished the occasion. At the time of the Empire it was said that the new-born child had been laid on a carpet decorated with a head of Julius Caesar. 'It's a fairy tale,' grumbled Madame Mère. 'We don't have carpets in our Corsican houses, even in winter, much less in summer.' L. Peretti: *Letizia*, and Lorenzo di Bradi: *La vraie figure de Bonaparte en Corse*.

† The Christian name Napoleon had belonged to a Bonaparte in the sixteenth century, but Letizia never mentioned this ancestor. 'My uncle died several weeks before the battle of Ponte Nuovo,' she used to say, 'but he came to Corte to fight. I gave my second son his name in memory of his heroism.' P. Bartel; *La jeunesse inédite de Napoléon*.

'I was a good patriot and Paolist to the core while the national government lasted,' he explained, 'but it doesn't exist any more. Now we are French. *Evviva il re e suo governo!*'*

The commander-in-chief of the French forces, the Comte de Marbeuf, governed the new province with an authority that was judged 'liberal and fruitful', carrying out to the letter the recommendations received from Versailles, namely: 'Find out how to gain the love of the Corsican people, and neglect nothing that can make them love France.' Carlo Buonaparte spoke French well; he had just submitted a thesis for his doctorate, belonged to a family with firm roots in the island, had ostentatiously abandoned the Paolist cause, possessed charming manners and was eager to be accepted: naturally he was received and listened to. For a young man trying to make his way in the world and satisfy his extravagant tastes, a chance to take part in the easy, brilliant life symbolised in Europe by the French Court was a godsend. And Madame Letizia, whose fresh beauty, a few weeks before, had been an ornament of Paoli's austere receptions in the fortress of Corte, was now about to be involved in the French society of the occupation, whose elegance represented the sunset glow of Louis XV's reign.

It was torture for a paralytically shy young woman, whose muteness discouraged attentions or even civility, to face the chatter of the salons when she so much preferred the solitude of the Casa Buonaparte, a tall convent-like house with a bare façade, in the heart of the most plebeian quarter of Ajaccio. There she felt truly at home, with her mother and mother-in-law, with her aunts living a stone's throw away, with her storeroom full of tidily stocked produce from her land – olives from Milelli, and Vitulo wine – while on the first floor could be heard the prattling of the two little boys, Joseph and Nabulio, and the muttering of Archdeacon Lucien. For, throughout her life, she valued nothing so much as her family, the company of her children and the simplicity of her old-fashioned way of life – a somewhat haughty

* J. Gregori: *Nouvelle histoire de la Corse.*

The House of the Bonaparte, Napoleon's birth place, at Ajaccio

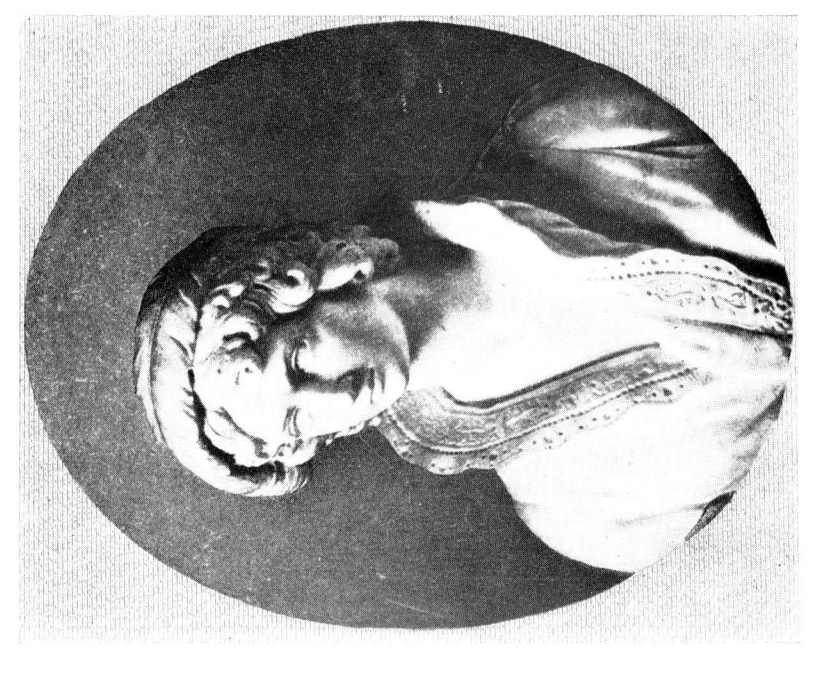

Letizia Bonaparte

Charles Bonaparte

'Beautiful as a Goddess'

simplicity, for when her cousin Maria Pozzo di Borgo, the lodger on the second floor, sprinkled one of the women of the family with dirty water, by emptying a receptacle out of the window, whether out of carelessness or on purpose, it led to a quarrel ending in the courts.*

Keeping house for an impecunious young barrister who had abandoned the law for politics and fashionable life, who liked good food and pretty women as well as fine clothes with French embroidery, was no sinecure, especially as the family steadily grew: a daughter, Maria-Anna was born and died in 1771, there was a still-born child in 1773, Lucien in 1775, Maria-Elisa in 1777, Louis in 1778, a child born and died in 1779, Pauline in 1780, Caroline in 1782 and Jerome in 1784. Thirteen children in all, of whom eight survived. To feed this family and entertain her husband's grand friends, Letizia and her two servants, Saveria and Caterina, helped by Nabulio's nurse Camillia Ilari, had to practise the utmost economy in order to make both ends meet.

Carlo Buonaparte's appointment as Assessor to the Royal Court of Justice at Ajaccio, with the functions of a judge and a salary of nine hundred *livres*, was not such a piece of good luck as the royal decree of 1770, by which Corsican gentry with titles and residences two centuries old were put on the same footing as the French nobility. To support his claim Carlo made the most of his Italian ancestors, who had been given patrician standing by the Grand Duke of Tuscany, and also of the affidavit of the Archbishop of Pisa at the time he received his doctorate, guaranteeing the relationship between the Italian and Corsican Buonapartes. His claim was allowed, he adopted the *particule,* signed himself as Charles de Buonaparte and was appointed to serve on a committee described as 'of the twelve noblemen', which carried with it

---

* This affair of the dirty water became a vendetta. Carlo Andrea Pozzo di Borgo, Napoleon's contemporary and sworn enemy, joined the Russian diplomatic service, persistently inflamed the Tsar against the Empire, entered Paris with the Allies after its defeat, took part in the Congress of Vienna, and finally became Russian Ambassador to London. His descendants built a chateau above Ajaccio out of the stones of Napoleon's palace, the Tuileries, burned in 1871.

another three hundred *livres*. It was not much, but the children's future was secure, as the King of France was obliged to grant them an education in keeping with their aristocratic birth.

The noble Madame Letizia de Buonaparte was now in her twentieth year. 'The elegance of her figure, her dazzling complexion and the regularity of her delicate features made her perfectly beautiful,' as a contemporary reports, adding maliciously, 'she was the most conspicuous woman in Ajaccio.'* A remark loaded with meaning, resonant with rumour – and what a bonus for the gossip-mongers of History! The insinuation was that Marbeuf could have got to know the young couple at Ajaccio, in 1764, the very year of their marriage . . . that he could have met Carlo and his wife again in 1768 . . . that he showered attentions on the young husband . . . that he took an interest in their children, and was godfather to Louis who was astonishingly like him . . . moreover, he was far from indifferent to young ladies even in his old age, and at seventy-one he was married again to a girl fifty-three years younger than himself . . . that he had a daughter in 1784 and a son in 1786, namely at the ages of seventy-two and seventy-four respectively, and that besides all this the Emperor Napoleon showed constant generosity to the members of the Marbeuf family, especially to the son, a second-lieutenant who would be his half-brother according to these calumnies . . . And above all, a conversation was recalled between Napoleon and his intimate friend Dr. Monge, on returning from Egypt.

'He embarked on the delicate question of his birth. Alluding to the well-known connection between his mother and M. de Marbeuf, governor of Corsica, and the latter's having befriended her children, he explained that he very much wanted to find out who was his real father . . . The reason he gave was his desire to know from whom he had inherited his military genius . . . Treating the subject as if it were a scientific problem he compared the dates of the governor's departure and of his own birth and

* J. V. Colchen, secretary to the governor of Corsica.

'Beautiful as a Goddess'

came to the conclusion that he was in fact Carlo's son. Twenty years later this seemed to be confirmed by his developing the same fatal disease, but at the time he couldn't understand whence came his talent for leading an army.'

So he was his father's son, and Madame Letizia's honour was saved ... As a Corsican writer commented wittily, Carlo de Buonaparte bequeathed his son his cancer and his beautiful grey eyes.* Everything else, according to Chateaubriand came to him 'by God's bounty'. Anyone possessed of common sense and goodwill might add a few words concerning the resemblance that existed between Napoleon and Joseph, which was so remarkable that after Waterloo the latter offered to impersonate the former, so that he could embark discreetly to the United States. And scandal-mongering could hardly go so far as to suggest that M. de Marbeuf could also have fathered Joseph, who – alas – had no aptitude at all for a military career.

On July 21, 1771, the young parents arranged to christen both Maria-Anna, at seven days old, and Nabulio who was nearly two and had only been privately baptized at birth. The future emperor's godfather was a certain Laurent Giubega (the King's prosecutor and deputy for Corsica, who had rallied to the French as promptly as Carlo de Buonaparte himself) and his godmother was his paternal aunt, Gertrude Paravicini. This family celebration only provided a brief harvest of happiness, and cruel trials were to follow for Madame Letizia. Little Maria-Anna died before the end of the year, and money troubles became more and more urgent; Carlo took it into his head to drag the Ramolinos before the courts for having failed to pay their daughter's dowry in full – and that ten years after the marriage. He won his suit and arranged to sell several humble objects belonging to his parents-in-law – barrels, buckets and wash-tubs in poor condition; and then, discovering that the price of a bullock had not been handed over, he returned to the attack and received another seventy *livres*. At the same time Archdeacon Lucien, who was a regular miser,

* J. Grégori. *Nouvelle histoire de la Corse.*

entered a suit against Carlo's mother, laying claim to the Casa Buonaparte, in which they both lived and ate at the same table! Letizia's natural pride, her sense of honour, and her submission to the head of the family like every Corsican wife, prevented her from mixing in these masculine affairs: she hid her troubles and maintained that impenetrable expression which was later to strike visitors to the Imperial Court; thus she forgot the present by concentrating on the future, in other words devoting herself to her children, of whom her son, Nabulio, deserved the nickname of *Ribulione*, or Hurricane, given him by his father, a hundred times a day.

'I was a quarrelsome imp,' admitted Napoleon later. 'Nothing impressed me. I was afraid of no one. I fought one, scratched another. They all respected me.'

In 1813, he was to say to the King of Rome, who celebrated his second birthday in the cosseted and respectful atmosphere of the Court:

'Lazy boy, at your age I was already fighting Joseph.'

Neither the lessons of the Convent Sisters of Ajaccio, devout girls who kept a mixed school for small children, nor the cane of his writing-master, the Abbé Recco, could pacify *Ribulione*. Violent, quick-tempered, aggressive, dominating and free with his hands, he was always in trouble. When they saw him running past with the other boys, his hair tousled, his eyes blazing and his clothes torn, the gossips burst out laughing: '*Napolione di mezza calzetta*'. One day some children from his school foolishly made up a song based on his name and the attentions he was paying one of the little girls:

> '*Napolione di mezza calzetta*
> *Fa l'amore a Giacometta*'*

They chose their time well! Nabulio chased them and gave them a thorough drubbing.

When he came home to the Casa Buonaparte, he had to give an

---

* Napolione, with his socks round his ankles, is making love to Giacometta.

'Beautiful as a Goddess'

account of himself to Madame Letizia, who wasn't taken in by his tales and didn't even laugh when Nabulio cunningly explained that he had dirtied his clothes playing at soldiers, or bartered his bread and jam for a military ration.

'Much use my smartness was to me; Mama Letizia wouldn't tolerate my escapades. Her tenderness was combined with severity, she punished naughtiness but rewarded goodness: nothing was missed,' he remembered.

It was Madame Letizia, and she alone, who successfully tamed what she called Nabulio's 'princely airs', in other words his taste for fighting pitched battles, joining groups to wander in the maquis, or engage in punitive expeditions which gave him a chance to exert his terribly strong will. She talked to him about honour, the family, the Corsican nation and religion, in the simple phrases of a woman of little education: the similarity between their characters accounted for the rest, and in the name of that morality Nabulio would accept a spanking when he missed mass, got soaked with rain to prepare himself for a soldier's career or made fun of his grandmother Fesch. This sternness was a good training for later life. When he was dying at St. Helena he remembered those early days, with melancholy affection.

'My excellent mother is a woman of spirit and many gifts. She has a man's character, proud and honourable. She deserves the deepest respect. The pride she taught me as a child affected my whole life. It is to my mother, it is to her good principles, that I owe my success and any good there is in me.'

'No one in the world has smacked so many kings and queens as I have,' Madame Letizia was to sum the matter up when she became Madame Mère.*

The children led a tough life of simple pleasures; there were happy days of riding on mule-back along stony tracks to some plot of ground belonging to the family, the vineyard at Sposata, the olive grove at Milelli, or some other mountain villages where the Buonapartes had spread their ramifications.

* L. Madelin: *La jeunesse de Bonaparte*.

'I see my youthful self among precipices, climbing high peaks or crossing deep valleys and narrow gorges, enjoying kindness and hospitality,' Nabulio would recall as Emperor. 'I always sided with my parents in the quarrels and vendettas they pursued to the seventh generation.'

Madame Letizia's outings were less concerned with the happiness of the children frisking round her mule than with the solution of some disagreement or other, or with getting a debt repaid.

'The family kept a communal bake-house where all the villagers came to grind their corn,' Napoleon remembered; these details delighted him, for he was as meticulous and economical as his mother. Grapes were vintaged, milk and goat cheese brought in; even butcher's meat wasn't paid for. They had an arrangement with the butcher by which they received it in exchange for an equivalent quantity of sheep, lambs, goats and even bullocks. The important thing was to spend no money. Money was very scarce.'

It was very scarce because Carlo had no idea of economising or even of keeping accounts, and one evening party – good food and fine clothes – would swallow up what the bake-house produced in a month. If only he had been like his wife, he could have lived well enough in an honourable provincial position. For even if money was short the family wasn't poor. 'Letizia owned a house at Santa Catalina, rented for 215 *livres*. The couple possessed two others, Badina and Badinella, bringing in 200 *livres*. The Vitullo vineyards (Letizia's) those of Maris Stella and La Candia (Archdeacon Lucien's), La Sposata (Carlo's) and Badicione, produced three hundred *louis* worth of excellent wine; the produce of their cornfields scattered round the town brought in 4000 *livres* every year, and there was 2000 in olive oil; added to which the sale of stock and fruit made a total of twelve or thirteen thousand *livres* – or about four or five million francs.'* Moreover, since the family had been ennobled they paid no taxes.

In order that Joseph and Nabulio could have a good education

* From £4000 to £5000. J. Grégori. *Nouvelle Histoire de la Corse.*

'Beautiful as a Goddess'

'on the Continent', bursaries were applied for, citing their four quarterings and the need to provide outfits ... a certificate of poverty drawn up without hesitation by Carlo, saying that he was 'poor and owned practically nothing except his salary as Assessor'.* The request was backed by M. de Marbeuf. Joseph was destined for the church and Nabulio for a military career; and their patrons – driven by Carlo's relentless solicitations – managed so well that it was arranged for both boys to travel with their father, who was to represent the Corsican nobility at Versailles, and so reduce expenses. They set off on December 17, 1778, and Madame Letizia could breathe again, after her prodigious efforts to equip her husband suitably for presentation at Court, and to get ready her sons' trousseaux for Autun. She went with them as far as Bastia in a carriage lent by M. de Marbeuf, and there she took leave of her husband, the boys and her half-brother, Joseph Fesch, who was to enter the seminary at Aix – a youth of sixteen whom she had brought up as a son and who was also going to be educated in 'the conquerors' school'. When she got back to Ajaccio she had to keep house alone and look after three-year-old Lucien, Elisa (who was just starting to walk) and Louis (a three month old baby), although money would not be forthcoming till the following summer, when she would be able to get something from her land.

A month later, Joseph Fesch, very proud of being chosen as one of the twenty Corsican scholars at Aix thanks to M. de Marbeuf's brother the bishop, had started on a clever rather than studious career; Carlo was going the rounds at Versailles; and the gentle and adaptable Joseph was popular with his school-mates. But Nabulio (whose Italian name was made fun of by the boys as

---

* The trousseau required for the school at Autun was very expensive. 'Three pairs of sheets to fit beds three feet wide and six long. Cutlery and a silver goblet engraved with the family arms, or monograms. Twelve napkins. A blue cloth coat with white buttons bearing the school's arms, and lining, collar and facings to match. Two pairs of black breeches made of Roman serge or worsted. A dozen shirts, a dozen handkerchiefs, two white collars, six cotton bonnets, two dressing-gowns, a bag of powder and a hair-ribbon, all new.'

'la paille au nez') 'doesn't join in with the rest. He's a simple, thoughtful character. He's usually alone, with an expression on his face as though already planning his future. I've only had him here three months. During that time he has learned enough French to talk easily and even write little essays and translation,' wrote one of his teachers, the Abbé Chardon. How often Madame Letizia used to grieve over the sufferings of that reserved, thoughtful little boy of nine, who would sometimes break out like a real savage. From Autun Nabulio soon passed into the seventh class of the Military College at Brienne. The trials he went through during those tough years may have influenced him later, when he took so much interest in education and created his own University. Oh if only Madame Letizia could have seen her child from dawn to dusk caught in the whirlpool life of a King's scholar: toilet, prayers, edifying books, mass, mathematics, physics, Latin, history, geography, fortifications, drawing, fencing, dancing, then living languages, evening prayers and bed. And all this at nine years old! The change in his life was so sudden, a mastery of the French language so hard to acquire, that Nabulio did not make a brilliant beginning at his studies and remained for some time at the bottom of the class. Then suddenly he threw himself on his books, filled his childish memory with chapters of history and geography and mathematical treatises, learned lists of logarithms by heart, devoured Plutarch and pondered over the lives of great men, took part in the performances given by the best pupils, even including a dancing interlude with sixteen other cadets.* Mama Letizia should have seen him now, elegantly dressed in his blue suit with white buttons, hurling himself into the daily struggle armed only with the principles she had taught him. An usher once tried to get him to eat his dinner on his knees on the tiled floor to punish him for some peccadillo.

---

* Napoleon never excelled at this form of amusement. In 1807 he asked the Countess Potocka what she thought of his dancing.
'Sire, for a great man you dance perfectly,' replied the young woman, who had a ready wit.

'Beautiful as a Goddess'

'I will dine standing up, Sir, and not on my knees. In my family we only kneel to God.'

His tormentor flung himself on him in a rage and the child burst into tears:

'Isn't that right, Mama? To God ... only to God?'*

Their reunion in 1782 was a great day for mother and son; it was more than three years since the parting at Bastia. Carlo de Buonaparte and his wife were coming to France, the first to consult doctors about his exhausting stomach ailment, the second to take the waters at Bourbonne-les-Bains, after the difficult birth of her daughter Caroline. Madame Letizia saw Versailles but was not dazzled by it. She came away from the most gorgeous palace in the world remembering only the tragically sad face of Marie-Antoinette, and hastened towards Brienne.

'When my mother came to see me,' Napoleon told General Montholon years later, 'she was so alarmed by my thinness and the way my face had altered, that she pretended I was a changeling and hardly recognised me for a few moments. I had in fact changed a lot, because I worked during recreation periods, and often spent the night going over the day's lesson. I couldn't tolerate the idea of not being top of the class, right from the start.'

He also remembered that his mother made a great impression on teachers and students alike ('at twenty-nine she was as beautiful as a goddess'), and that he suggested to her that he might go into the navy, but she set her face against the idea – and by so doing probably changed the course of history.

When she got back to Ajaccio Madame Letizia found more troubles awaiting her; Carlo's illness had made him irritable and unreliable, and he launched into new transactions which hung fire and left him short of money. This was the moment Nabulio chose to write his father a famous letter.†

---

* R. Peyre. *Napoléon Ier et son temps*.

† Challenged by some historians, this letter or another in the same vein must have been written for Nabulio to receive his mother's letter of June 2, 1784, which is universally held to be authentic.

'If you or my patrons cannot give me the means to maintain a more reputable appearance in this school, send for me to come home, and that as soon as possible; I'm tired of looking like a beggar and seeing my insolent fellow pupils, who have only their wealth to recommend them, mocking at my poverty.'

Carlo was at Bastia and the letter was opened and answered by Madame Letizia, who wrote:

'I have received your letter, my son, and if the handwriting and signature hadn't proved it was from you, I would never have believed you were the author of it. You are the best loved of my children, but if I ever get a similar letter from you again, I will have nothing more to do with Napoleon. Where did you learn, young man, that a son could address his father as you have done, whatever plight he may find himself in? You can thank heaven that your father was away from home ... As for your needs, even if you have the right to tell us about them, you should also have realised that our complete inabiilty to help you was the cause of our silence. It is neither because of the unsuitable suggestion you dared to make, nor your threats, that I am sending you a letter of credit for 300 francs on the Bahie bank. My sending this money will show you how much we love our children. Napoleon, I trust that in future you will behave with more discretion and affection, so that I shall never again have to write as I have just done. Now, as before, I remain

Your affectionate mother
Letizia Buonaparte
Ajaccio, June 2, 1784.'

At the beginning of the year, Carlo had to travel to Paris again to take his eldest daughter, Elisa, to Saint-Cyr, the convent school established by Madame de Maintenon; he had to borrow 25 *louis* for the purpose. He took Lucien to Brienne, and visited Nabulio; and as if he suspected that his days were numbered, he multiplied his efforts on behalf of Joseph, who refused outright to become a priest and wanted to serve in the artillery. When he

'Beautiful as a Goddess'

started home to Ajaccio he was so ill that he hadn't the strength to make a detour to Brienne and embrace Nabulio and Lucien for the last time. Madame Letizia was pregnant with her last child – Jerome, future King of Westphalia – and she was appalled to see her ailing husband, crippled with debts and 'reduced to penury' as he called it, pack his trunks again at the end of the year to go to Paris, with the vague plan of pursuing some troublesome and long-standing suit against the Jesuits. But if Carlo said he would do a thing he did it, so here he was travelling the French roads, and stopping at Montpellier – which at this time possessed the best school of medicine in France – to consult doctors; he fell ill, took to bed at the house of friends (the wife being a Corsican) and died in February 1785, at the age of thirty-nine, in the presence of his son Joseph and Joseph Fesch, who heard him whisper at the last minute:

'I wish I could have seen my little Napoleon.'

Why Nabulio more than the others? It is almost as if the terrible destiny of that exceptional being was already having its effect, even on his own family.

It was Joseph's task to take the sad news to Letizia, now a widow in her thirties, who had given birth thirteen times and had eight children to care for.* After five years at Brienne, Nabulio had been for several months in the Royal Military Academy in Paris; he wrote his mother one of those letters of condolence for which shy adolescents show so little gift:

March 29, 1785.

My dear Mother,

Today, now that time has calmed the first passion of my grief, I hasten to express my gratitude for the goodness you have always shown us. Be comforted, dearest Mother; circumstances demand it.

We shall redouble our care and gratitude, and will be happy if

---

* 'If my father had lived', said Napoleon, 'my mother could have had twenty children.'

our obedience can make up a little for the incalculable loss of a beloved husband. I must end now, dear Mother, my sorrow forces me, and I implore you to calm your own. I am in perfect health, and I pray every day that heaven may grant you the same . . . .

Your very humble and loving son
Napoleone de Buonaparte.

P.S. The Queen of France gave birth to a prince, the Duke of Normandy, at seven in the evening of March 27.'

Years afterwards, at St. Helena, he remembered this first sorrow and spoke of it to his Corsican doctor, Antommarchi: 'Left alone, without anyone to guide or support her, my mother had to manage everything herself. But her strength was equal to the burden. She supervised everything, organised everything with a wisdom and shrewdness quite exceptional in a woman of her age. Ah! doctor, what a woman!'

And with cool lucidity he underlined the consequences this death had on his own career:

'If my father had lived he would probably have brought an end to my career. He would have been a deputy at the Constituent Assembly, taken the side of the intriguers, the Lameths, the Noailles; he would have been obliged to launch me into the world too young. I would not have been able to gain the success that I have won. My father was a patriot, but clung to his ideas about the nobility.'

II
'The Widow Buonaparte'

Widowhood reduced Madame Letizia to a barely adequate income of 1000 to 1200 *livres* a year, with four of her children holding bursaries in the schools of the King of France.* 'Still young and beautiful, surrounded by general esteem,' wrote her biographer the Baron Larrey, she could easily have remarried had she wanted to, in spite of thirteen confinements, eight surviving children, and modest resources. She was advised to take a husband rich enough to secure her children's future and improve her own position. She nobly refused the offers that were made her. She refused, because Joseph was already a young man, and took his role as head of the family seriously, and did his best to collect the revenues from their land, while all Nabulio's letters spoke of the officer's commission which would make him independent.

'I was an officer at the age of sixteen years and two weeks' he used to remember, proudly and with good reason! In September 1785 the cadet de Buonaparte, the first Corsican to be admitted to the Royal Military Academy, was in fact passed in his examination as second-lieutenant by the famous mathematician and physicist Laplace. Destined for the regiment of La Fère, now garrisoned at Valence, he left Paris on October 30 to start the career we know so well, and which was admirably summed up when he exclaimed at St. Helena:

'What a romance my life has been!'

* From £500 to £600 a year.

Sixteen years old, the uniform of an artilleryman – the smartest of them all, he often said as Emperor – eight hundred *livres* pay a year, plus twenty-five as billeting allowance and a pension of two hundred from the Military College, as well as a commission in one of the best French regiments. Small wonder that Napoleon wrote later: 'I remember my time at Valence with pleasure.' Instruction, manoeuvres, tactics or exercises in the polygon, all delighted him. He was billeted on a Mademoiselle Bou, who washed his linen and mended his stockings; he spent his evenings with Aurel the bookseller, who lent him books; he dined at the Trois Pigeons inn, went to bed at ten and got up at four, and his dreams in his modest second-lieutenant's bedroom were more probably about the house at Ajaccio and his native land than about the girl he had enjoyed the disturbing pleasure of picking cherries with.

'I drew my very existence from Corsica,' he wrote at the time, 'and with it a violent love for my unfortunate country and its independence. I too wanted to be a Paoli!'*

A man of contradictions, he later declared:

'I think of Brienne as my native land; it was there that I received my first impressions as a man.'

In April 1786 he embarked on a manuscript about his island and his hero Paoli, and in the following month he produced an *Essay on Suicide*, presumably inspired by the despair into which the former work had plunged him.

'What shall I find in my homeland? My compatriots loaded with chains, trembling as they kiss the oppressor's hand?'

There was in fact much to discourage and confuse a man, who cherished the ambition of making a career among his fellow-countrymen, and dreamed only of a free Corsica. But what youthful candour on the part of an adolescent singled out by Fate – or, as he would say, circumstances and public opinion – to become one of the most powerful men of his day!

---

* Napoléon: *Nouvelle Corse*.

'The Widow Buonaparte'

In January 1786 he asked for leave and it was granted. He set off in September, going by way of Aix to see his uncle Fesch and his brother Lucien, and disembarked at Ajaccio on the fifteenth, after eight years of absence, wearing the royal blue uniform with scarlet facings which he was to make so famous. Was Corsica in truth his native land? Sentimentally speaking yes, no doubt, but Madame Letizia was quick to realise that her Nabulio had become completely French: his luggage was stuffed with books by writers she had never heard of – Montaigne, Voltaire, Montesquieu and Rousseau.

'Family worries darkened the years of my youth, made me serious before my time,' Napoleon explained later.

Serious he most certainly was, and he soon took over the position of head of the family in place of Joseph, whose easy-going character and cheerful rotundity barely concealed his indolence; but he had to give up political ambition for a while and devote himself entirely to the domestic affairs at present submerging Madame Letizia; he had to be responsible for the family property, for Archdeacon Lucien (who was quite incapable) and his young brothers and sisters. And all this was done strictly and conscientiously.

'It was impossible to argue with him,' grumbled Lucien one day; 'he was annoyed by the smallest comment, and lost his temper at the slightest resistance.'

Madame Letizia was amazed – though her admiration was mingled with fear – at Nabulio's efforts to bring in a little money by checking debtors' accounts, badgering shepherds and farmers, and firmly applying for help from the royal providential administration. He actually made her sign a letter to the King's Commissioner, ending with the words: 'As far as is possible, you will have made good your predecessor's false speculations, and you will have benefited my family by observing the strictest rules of justice. This sort of chance does not arise every day, Monseigneur: make the most of it, and if your suppliant recognises your goodness by the liveliest gratitude, you, Monseigneur, owe to her the fact that you will never think of this family without inner satisfaction.'

The affair concerned some mulberry orchards planted by Carlo de Buonaparte, which would be the better for government help. Buonaparte, Lieutenant of Artillery, claimed 3050 *livres* 'on behalf of Madame his mother'. He received no reply, but Madame Letizia declared that her husband's litigious temperament had been inherited by Nabulio, when her son told her he had asked for five and a half months' additional leave 'with pay, in consideration of his slender means and medical expenses' – actually so as to go in person to Paris to obtain satisfaction.

The house was now without a head, and the children – Louis (aged ten), Pauline (eight), Caroline (six) and Jerome (four) – may well have sighed with relief at being free from their brother's stern guardianship. Joseph was at Pisa studying for a doctorate in law, and a letter written to him by Madame Letizia at this time gives a glimpse of the humble standard of life at the Casa Buonaparte:

'My dearest son,
Your uncle's letter will tell you what you must do. He wants you to get your doctorate. You know the present state of the family affairs, and it is needless to ask you to spend as little as possible. We have no servant. Do what you can to bring one back with you. I would like an experienced woman – not too young, over forty, to work in the house (not the fields), and do the washing if possible; if she doesn't want to, no matter, but she must do our simple cooking, be able to sew and iron, and be religious. That is what I would like, because since my trouble with my finger I cannot sew a single stitch. You'll want to know what wages you can give her, and my answer is: the least possible, but as a guide I would say three or four francs a month; if she's good, twenty sous more or less make no difference, for I need her badly . . . Your sisters and brothers embrace you, and ask you to bring them each a straw hat for the summer. Grandmamma,

Bonaparte in 1797

Bonaparte, Lieutenant of Artillery

Madame Mère and bust of Napoleon

'The Widow Buonaparte'

Mamuccia, Caterina and your uncles and aunts all send greetings. I too embrace you and wish you a happy return. Don't forget anything I say in my letter.'

After Nabulio's return the tone of the letters changes – the lion has left his mark – and the correspondence with the Corsican Commission starts again, dealing with the orchard, payments due to clients, and the hoped-for subsidy, as well as complaining of lack of business and scanty profits. 'I dare to hope that you might help me a little by allowing me the cost of the trees delivered; this seems to me only fair and has also been authorised by the minister; I should trespass on your amiability if I detailed all the wrongs I have suffered in this affair; I must therefore rely on your generosity.'

Madame Letizia and Nabulio tried every means they could think of to collect a little pocket money to send to Lucien, at school at Aix, and to Joseph, who was up to every sort of wild behaviour at Pisa. At last they succeeded in getting paid for the mulberry trees, but were unable to persuade the Commissioner to order a bog to be drained from which they had hoped for considerable profits. And time was passing! Nabulio had been on leave for twenty months – the Royal administration would be thought very tolerant today – and was due to rejoin his regiment at Auxonne, where it had been since December 1787. Another request from Madame Letizia to the Minister for War may well have travelled in his luggage in June 1788.

'The widow de Buonaparte, of Ajaccio in Corsica, has the honour to implore your indulgence so that her fourth son, Louis, may be admitted to one of the military schools. He competed in 1787 without success, but was promised a chance at the following year's examination when he would still be of the right age; this has now taken place but you have felt obliged to give preference to children whose family qualifications are presumably solider, and he has once more been refused, leaving him without any hope for the next examination ... With the responsibility for educating eight children, the widow of a man who always served the King in the administration of the isle of Corsica and spent considerable sums in support of the government's plans, implores your help at the foot of the throne and from your sympathetic generosity. The voices of the eight children will carry her prayers for your safe-keeping to Heaven, Monseigneur.'

Nabulio found life at Auxerre hard. 'I go to bed at ten,' he wrote, 'and get up at four. I eat only one meal a day, and don't dine until three o'clock.' A few years later he was to reply tartly to an official of the Empire who complained of his poor pay:

'Monsieur, when I had the honour to be a second-lieutenant, I breakfasted off dry bread but I kept my poverty hidden behind locked doors.'

Yet another of Madame Letizia's lessons!

Meanwhile he devoured book after book – works on Assyria, Persia, Egypt and Rome, Plato, Machiavelli, Racine and Corneille, the Constitutions of Athens and Sparta. He recorded and stored all this knowledge in his fabulous memory. One day when he was under arrest he plunged into Justinian's *Institutiones*, and fifteen years later was able to quote whole pages from it at a Council of State.

On June 20, 1789 (the day of the Oath of the Tennis-court), the States General convoked by Louis XVI decided to give the Kingdom a constitution and Nabulio declared with intelligent and youthful confidence:

'Revolutions are good for military men of spirit and courage.'

On July 14, 1789, came the fall of the Bastille; on August 4 the abolition of privileges – a measure which at last gave an opportunity to the lesser nobility like the Buonapartes; but Madame Letizia, terrified by the news that aristocrats serving in the King's army were emigrating, wrote to her son begging him not to 'cross the Rhine' – which he can have had no intention of doing, since he had just written a strange and fervent letter to Paoli, 'the friend' whom all the Buonapartes had turned their backs on so promptly:

'General,

I was born during my Country's death-agony, with thirty thousand Frenchmen debouching on our shores and drowning the throne of liberty in torrents of blood; such was the odious spectacle that first met my eyes; the cries of the dying, the groans of the oppressed and tears of the desperate surrounded my cradle from birth... When you left our island, you took with you all hope of happiness.'

No doubt Nabulio was mainly concerned with presenting the manuscript of his *Letters from Corsica* to the 'patriot'... Perhaps he wanted to be held in reserve to further the cause of local independence, and was aiming at becoming the second great man of his small country.

The political, economic and social ideas of the French Revolution were bound to awaken the Corsican demons of the past: revolts broke out at Ajaccio on August 15, 1789, and the devout Madame Letizia must have felt sickened to see Monseigneur Doria, the bishop, insulted, spat and jeered upon as he was dragged through the streets. Fortunately two deputies saved the situation and staved off civil war by proposing the formation of a National Committee, to communicate the desires of the population to the Assembly at Versailles. Gaffori, son of a friend of Paoli's, became second in command to the governor, and occupied Ajaccio at the head of a regiment and five companies.

'The son has come to bring back the despotism put an end to by his father of glorious memory,' jeered Nabulio, who had just arrived for another six months' furlough.

So Madame Letizia was drawn into the political whirlpool against her will, just as in the darkest days of the Paolist resistance against the French. And here was Nabulio calling a meeting of the inhabitants of Ajaccio and framing a document for them to send to the Assembly at Versailles.

'Seigneurs, we lost everything when we lost our liberty, and we have gained nothing but humiliation and tyranny from the rule of your compatriots. A vast nation is awaiting to receive its happiness from you; we are a part of it, we are more troubled than the rest; cast your eyes in our direction, or we shall perish.'

After a fresh revolt had broken out, at Bastia this time, the Chamber of Deputies gave in.

'The island of Corsica is declared to be a part of the French Empire; its inhabitants will be ruled by the same Constitution as all other Frenchmen. From this moment the King will be asked to transmit thither, and make public, all the decrees passed by the National Assembly.'

So on December 4, Louis XVI signed a document, granting Paoli and other exiles the right to return to their island, and Madame Letizia was teased by Joseph and Nabulio into making large cotton banners bearing legends such as '*Vive La Nation*', '*Vive Paoli*', or '*Vive Mirabeau*' (who had fathered the decree of pardon). She was not, however, over-eager to share their fine enthusiasms, for she knew very well that Paoli would never forgive Carlo's sons for their father's volte-face ...

On July 17 the great man landed, while the bells of all the steeples rang and the crowds shouted themselves hoarse:

'*Evviva il Babbo della Patria!*'

His supporters had already invented a slogan: 'He is the one; our native land and the constitution depend on him in person.'

Maybe, but in Corsica unanimity, or even a simple majority, is hard to come by. Joseph and Nabulio hurried to meet their hero, only to be coolly received, and in the municipal elections that followed soon after, Joseph was set aside in favour of a staunch Paolist candidate. It was therefore with a heart full of anger that Nabulio re-embarked for France in January 1791, taking with him his brother Louis, whose education he had undertaken to be responsible for out of his lieutenant's pay. It was a short stay, for he was home again in September, having taken it into his head to get Joseph elected deputy for Corsica. Very opportunely, Archdeacon Lucien died on October 16, 1791, and the Buonaparte clan

'The Widow Buonaparte'

found themselves richer by the sum they needed for an electoral campaign – not for Joseph this time, but for Nabulio who had decided to get himself made Lieutenant-Colonel of the Corsican National Guard. The Casa Buonaparte became the headquarters of work and revelry, and Madame Letizia soon saw their inheritance melting away before her eyes. But when it came to an argument she was won over.

'The only person to whom Napoleon opened his heart, with whom he discussed his affairs, whom he tried to convince, revealing his plans and motives, the only person he would listen to quietly, who could force him to account for his occasionally bizarre and extravagantly original behaviour, was his mother,' we are told by a contemporary witness, Judge Nasica. 'He told me her powers of thinking and reasoning were of the highest. "My mother could govern a kingdom; she has excellent judgement and never makes a mistake. Her experience and advice are extremely useful to me."'

'I'm nearly at the end of my tether,' this woman of excellent judgement confessed one morning, 'and unless I sell or borrow ... It's not poverty I'm afraid of, it's the disgrace.'

'Mother, I implore you to take heart and try and support me to the end. We must keep on, we've gone too far to draw back.'*

And also much too far not to be dangerously exposed. Right from the start Paoli made life difficult for Lieutenant-Colonel Napoleon de Buonaparte; there was trouble between the people of Ajaccio and even between the troops of the new Lieutenant-Colonel, the Paolists and the King's forces ... Nabulio was threatened with dismissal in his native town and with arrest at Valence for not having rejoined his regiment after his leave was up. In May 1792 Madame Letizia urged him to return to France. Did she realise that the island was too small a field of action for this turbulent genius, or was she afraid for his life? The wisdom she was to show throughout her long career was based on her deep primitive instincts as a woman and a mother.

* P. Bartel: *La jeunesse inédite de Napoléon.*

In Paris on June 20, 1792, Nabulio witnessed the taking of the Tuileries and the fall of the monarchy.

'*Che coglione!*'* he exclaimed, of Louis XVI. 'How on earth could he let that rabble in? They should have mowed down four or five hundred with gunfire and the rest would still be running.'

The School of St. Cyr was a victim of the turmoil of revolution and had to close its doors. In September Nabulio was granted leave and the expenses of the journey, to take his sister Elisa back to Corsica. The military administration of sansculottes was quite as liberal as the King's.

There was great joy at the Casa Buonaparte where in October the whole family were reunited, but Nabulio, true to character, frowned when he heard what had been happening in the island.

Paoli had intrigued to prevent Joseph standing for the Convention, and had even refused to take on Lucien as a secretary – Lucien who had left school at Aix endowed with Jacobin eloquence, quoting Greek and Roman writers and talking of Brutus, Caesar, Marius and Sulla. Nor was Nabulio's uniform as an officer in the pay of the Revolution likely to mollify the old nationalist patriot, for Fortune was to favour the plans of Madame Letizia's sons ... After the death of Louis XVI, Paoli was imprudent enough to contact Admiral Hood, Commander-in-Chief in the Mediterranean, with the purpose of putting the island under the protection of Great Britain, and this was his downfall. He was denounced and summoned to Paris to defend himself, but he ignored the order and the Convention sent three commissioners to investigate, while the eighteen-year old orator Lucien was furiously abusing 'the man who wants to hand Corsica over to the English'. The revolutionary machine was at work: Paoli was formally accused, and Lucien wrote triumphantly to his family: 'There is a warrant out for his arrest ... Our fortunes are made.' What a rash young man! His letter was intercepted at Ajaccio and taken to Paoli, who seethed with rage!

* What a fool!

'The Widow Buonaparte'

'*Che bricconcello* ... The dirty little scoundrel.'

There was no need to be as learned as Nabulio or Lucien to realise that danger was now at the very doors of the family home and that revenge would be pitiless. Madame Letizia understood her compatriots and trembled for her sons. Nabulio escaped an ambush, was arrested by the Paolists, but succeeded in escaping to Bastia where Joseph was waiting with troops faithful to the revolutionary government. Madame Letizia tried to face the situation by barricading herself inside the Casa Buonaparte with her mother, Joseph Fesch and the five children, but during the night of May 24 to 25 a friend from the mountains called Costa came to warn her of approaching danger.

'Hurry, Signora, hurry ... The brigands are close behind us. It's you they want. There's not a moment to lose. Leave at once; my men and I will defend you.'*

Madame Letizia was not taken unawares, as a few days earlier Nabulio had managed to get a note to her, which amounted to marching orders. '*Preparatevi, queste paĕse non e per noi.*'† She had already entrusted her family papers to a cousin and hidden her two youngest children, Pauline and Jerome, with their maternal grandmother. She got up quickly that night, barely had time to give a last look round her beloved house, at Carlo's study, at her old uncle's invalid chair, while she helped the children get dressed. They left furtively in the inky darkness, meaning to take refuge in the Milelli property, since Costa told them that the danger would not last long; all the Corsicans who were against occupation by the English were under arms and marching towards the ports; Nabulio would arrive by ship at Ajaccio any day with four hundred men and that would be the end of Paoli and his band of traitors. Alas! hardly had they settled in at Milelli when a friend, the Abbé Coti, arrived out of breath on horseback, and announced that the Casa Buonaparte had been pillaged, that

---

* Napoleon remembered this action, which saved his family from massacre, by leaving in his will: 'To Costa of Bastelica in Corsica, 100,000 francs'.

† Get ready, this country is not for us.

the Paolists were on the tracks of the fugitives, who must be ready for anything. Their safest refuge would be the Capitello tower, where they could await Nabulio's arrival.

The Genoese tower of Capitello stands in the Gulf of Ajaccio opposite one of the most beautiful views in the world, looking ont ou to the îles Sanguinaires as they turn red at dusk, and at green hills planted with orange trees and mimosas. One reaches it by a difficult path, first across the marsh of the Campo dell'Oro with its innumerable bog-holes, and then the awkward stream of the Prunelli swollen by melting snows and rain. Poor Madame Letizia, how often I have imagined her plight, as I followed in her tracks on this nocturnal excursion, at a time when chance made me an inhabitant of that same tower! I imagine her dressed all in black, sitting bolt upright on her horse, tightly embracing her children who are riding pillion, Costa's men leading the way and Bocognano's friends bringing up the rear, Pauline whimpering.

'Don't cry. Do as I do, I suffer in silence.'

They reached the tower standing alone in the middle of a field of asphodels that covered the rocky spur dominating the stone-sprinkled beach. Two intolerable days of waiting, their eyes scanning the horizon for a sight of sails bringing Nabulio and his friends, and wondering whether they would really come.* They ate and slept on the beaten earth. They waited. They prayed. They hoped. And then on May 30, after six days of suspense, there was a sound of gunfire... The French squadron anchored off Ajaccio opened fire on the citadel, which responded. Sails were unfurled. The ships veered broadside on, preparing to withdraw and find a place to land. A xebec moved off towards Capitello. A

* Anything was possible, even Nabulio's disappearance, for Paoli's vendetta had taken shape in a threatening decree: 'In consideration of the fact that the Buonaparte brothers, born in the mire of despotism and brought up under the care and at the expense of a lustful pasha, have supported treachery by joining with the Commissaries of the Convention, they are hereby abandoned to their own remorse and public opinion, which now and henceforth condemns them to perpetual execration and infamy.'

'The Widow Buonaparte'

boat was lowered. Madame Letizia stifled a cry of joy, as she recognised a thin figure in a blue coat. At last! It was Nabulio.

They fell into one another's arms. Then they hurriedly embarked and put out to sea. Next day was the first stage of what was already exile – at Calvi, where they stayed with Laurent Giubega, Nabulio's godfather. Caroline and Jerome rejoined their mother there, having made the journey across country. After debating the situation they decided that the game was up, that they would go to France, trying to get past the English ships cruising round the island waiting to see what would be the result of the struggle between the French and the Paolists. They embarked therefore on the corvette *Belette*, and on June 13, 1793, landed at Toulon:

'Buonaparte, Letizia, seamstress, 56 years old,*
passport No 576
Buonaparte, Marianne, seamstress, 18 years old,
passport No 577
Buonaparte, Paulette, seamstress, 15 years old,
passport No 578
Buonaparte, Anontiata (sic), seamstress, 13 years old,
passport No 579
Buonaparte, Jerome, schoolboy, 11 years old,
passport No 580
Fesch, Joseph, Archdeacon of Ajaccio, 30 years old.'

* This was an error. Madame Letizia was only about 43 years old. As for the children they have all added two years to their ages. Under the Empire the Christian names of the girls – Marianne, Paulette and Anontiata became Elisa, Pauline and Caroline (which have been used throughout this book to avoid confusion).

III
'Madame Letizia Buonaparte, seamstress'

The Convention granted meagre subsidies to Corsican patriots seeking refuge in France: Madame Letizia would receive 75 *livres* a month and 50 *livres* for each of her children, in all about £80 a month.

'My mother reached Marseilles expecting to find patriotism and a welcome worthy of all the sacrifices she had made,' growled Napoleon at St. Helena. 'She barely found safety.'

At Toulon, where she first took refuge, the family was intimidated by the atmosphere of terror, created and kept going by a handful of dubious revolutionaries and freed convicts, who detained, tortured and hanged anyone they suspected and everyone with a *de* to his name. Nabulio rejoined his regiment at Nice, but was soon posted to the ammunition store at Avignon. Madame Letizia thought it safer to settle at La Valette, a village perched among the hills surrounding the town, where she occupied two rooms on the second floor of a house near the church, which can still be seen. A few weeks later the great port was surrounded by Admiral Hood's forces 'in the name of the King of France', and they had to pack up again. This time they chose Méounes, a village near Brignoles, where she lived on loans from sympathetic neighbours, for which she had to pay a high interest, as the subsidies from the Convention no longer arrived. When the family saw that they were in danger of being caught between the pincers of the English army and the revolutionary patriots, they took to the road once more and hurried towards Marseilles.

Deprived of its trade by the war, Marseilles now offered few openings. Madame Letizia was unable to find work, and had nothing to live on but the small sums Nabulio sent her; she made her family lead a simple, even austere existence. This did not prevent calumnies later on when Nabulio was Emperor, and his family were accused of having lived on what the daughters earned by their charms; however the narrative of a Corsican servant, engaged at the beginning of 1794 when the situation was beginning to improve thanks to Joseph and Nabulio, was to give the lie to these rumours: Madame Letizia did her own modest shopping and the girls cooked when they got back from the school they went to with Jerome. Who could suspect, as they saw this group of children chaperoned by a severe-looking lady in black, that a procession of future kings and queens was passing by?

Soon afterwards the family were again united, and could tell each other of their achievements. Joseph had been appointed Commissary for war, Louis had passed his examination into the artillery. Lucien's eloquence had gained him a reputation among the revolutionaries of St. Maximin, and Nabulio was given the command of the artillery besieging Toulon. It was like a fairy tale, and the family were grateful to the chief author of their success, Saliceti, former deputy for Corsica and Joseph's fellow-student at the University of Pisa, now serving in the Midi. Thanks to him they were also able to take over the requisitioned house of an émigré – the Hôtel de Cyprières, and this soon became the meeting place for smart officers, townsmen, and politicians proud of knowing friends of Saliceti's.

In December Nabulio drove the English out of Toulon and was promoted Brigadier-General at the age of twenty-four. He was already famous and his mother was a person of importance in Marseilles. When he was appointed Inspector of the Coast, with headquarters at Nice, he settled in the Château Sallé at Antibes, and his first action was to send for his mother and sisters to join him.

This large Provençal house with its red tiles can still be seen, looking out over the Mediterranean from its park full of mimosas and orange-trees. Here the young general's staff was established under the direction of Junot and Marmont. What happy and prosperous times seemed to be beginning for the family! Joseph had just married Marie-Julie Clary, ugly but fabulously rich daughter of a Marseilles merchant, and came on a visit with his young wife. Elisa, Caroline and Pauline lavished attentions on visitors to the house, among whom was Charlotte Robespierre, sister of the ruler of France . . . their luck had certainly come back. But Madame Letizia – simple, economical, even mistrustful as ever – still washed her own linen in the stream, repeating words that were to become famous:

'If it only lasts!'

And it didn't last. Suddenly she was torn between Nabulio and Lucien, the former reproaching the latter for marrying the daughter of the innkeeper where he lodged, without asking the permission of his family.* She had to mollify Pauline whose forty-year-old and far from rich suitor, 'citizen Billon', had been sent packing by Nabulio. And now, on Thermidor 9, came the fall of the 'tyrant' Robespierre; his execution and also that of his brother, who was a friend and patron of Nabulio. A breathing-space for France, but not for the Buonapartes. Nabulio was arrested and imprisoned, first at Nice then at Antibes, and when released six days later he was deprived of his command. Struck off the lists of the artillery by the Committee of Public Safety, he was however transferred to the infantry and given command of the Army of the West, at present engaged against the Royalist *Chouans*. He was in no hurry to take over his new functions, and went to Paris, where he, Junot and Marmont and his brother Louis shared a tiny apartment in the rue de la Huchette, and lived on a few sous a day, apparently awaiting a change in their luck.

* To gain his desire, Lucien, who was not yet nineteen, had used Napoleon's birth certificate, and wrote to him saying merely: 'I have found a poor and virtuous girl, and married her.'

'Madame Letizia Buonaparte, seamstress'

Madame Letizia was now left quite without support and had to retreat to Marseilles, where she and Joseph lived at the expense of the Clary family. They hardly had time to breathe before news of Lucien's troubles reached them. The former president of the Revolutionary Committee of St. Maximin was accused of being Robespierre's henchman, committed for trial, and imprisoned at Aix. Lucien, with his charming refined features, his gentle myopic gaze and his delicate health, not to mention his taste for flowery language and poetry, was a favourite with his mother, who at once, in the best Corsican tradition, appealed to one of her compatriots, an influential representative on service with the army in Italy.

'Having none of his brothers with me here, and not knowing where to turn, I am writing to you in the hope that, as a friend, you will do something for him ... I cannot imagine what they have against him, since there have been no émigrés in this region and no one has perished under the blade of the law. Only a few have been arrested, and those had been denounced; I do not know why.'

One can picture her struggling with the diabolical difficulties of the French language, twisting her letters to suit the fashion of the day and stuffing them with revolutionary phrases. She managed to get 500 francs to her *caro Luciano* through a friend at Aix – it was a large sum for a woman with no fixed income. Lucien was released on August 5, but Nabulio had refused to take up his post in the West, and his name was struck off the list of generals: he was so short of cash that this rude blow knocked him momentarily off his feet. His mother at once wrote him one of the letters that give us some idea of the toughness of her character: 'It is fine and noble to rise above the reverses of fortune. What would you think if I told you that this event may perhaps be all for the best; that the decree proscribing you may turn out to be your passport to brilliant honours in the future and gain you a high reputation.'

The element of the miraculous played an important part in the life of this quietly confident woman, and, like Napoleon, she could compare her life to a novel. On October 5, less than five months after this crisis in the lives of her two sons, a royalist rebellion broke out in Paris, and Barras, Commander-in-Chief for the Interior, bethought himself of the little General Buonaparte whom he had caught sight of during the siege of Toulon, and sent for him.

'You're in command of the artillery.'

This pocket-size general, with his straight hair framing a pale but serious face, whose enemies were to call him 'General Vendémiaire' in memory of the occasion, shot down the rioters on the steps of the church of St. Roch, saved the Convention, strengthened Barras's position and was made General-in-Chief of the Army of the Interior. Once more, his first thought was for his relations. 'The family lack for nothing,' he wrote to Joseph. 'I have sent them money, promissory notes, fine clothes. They have plenty of everything.' Nor was that the end of his efforts for them: Joseph was made a consul, Lucien Commissary for War, and Louis aide-de-camp to the General Commander-in-Chief of the Interior. Madame Letizia took over some handsome rooms at Marseilles, where they went on as before, entertaining and giving balls until the day when, like a thunder-clap, they heard the news of Nabulio's marriage. And what a marriage!

It was like a scene from a comedy. It took place on March 9, 1796, as night fell in the registry office of the second *arrondissement* in Paris. Josephine and her witnesses – one of them her lover, Barras – waited for the bridegroom for a whole hour – for two hours indeed. The candles were burning low. A sound of steps. Buonaparte rushed in like a whirlwind, followed by his aide-de-camp, and awoke the registrar:

'Come, Monsieur, be quick and marry us.'

'Marie-Josephe-Rose Tascher,* born in the island of Martinique in the Windward Islands,' who had reduced her age by four years,

* On the marriage certificate there is no mention of 'de la Pagerie', probably because titles had been dropped during the Revolution.

was now quite unconsciously entering history, and also the Buonaparte clan, which must have alarmed her for it was no trifling matter. Josephine's notary Raguideau said to his client in amazement: 'You're making a great mistake; you'll regret it; it's folly to marry a man who has nothing but his name and his sword.'*

Forty-eight hours later Napoleon Bonaparte had been appointed Commander-in-Chief of the army in Italy, and was hurrying towards his destiny, towards the ragged 37,000 with whose help he was to crush the Austrians, sending his wife from every stopping-place letters worthy to take their place in any anthology of amorous literature. 'Not a day has passed without my loving you. Not a night without my holding you in my arms. I have not drunk a cup of tea without cursing the glory and ambition that keeps me away from my life's soul. Whether I am immersed in affairs, at the head of my troops or surveying my encampments, my adorable Josephine alone occupies my heart and mind, absorbs my thoughts. If I leave you with the speed of the torrential Rhône, it is so that I can return to you the sooner. If I get up to work in the middle of the night, it is because by doing so I may see my sweet love a few days earlier.'

'How funny this Bonaparte is!' exclaimed the loved one.

'Bonaparte' – no longer 'Buonaparte'. The last time he signed his name in its Italian form of 'Napolione Buonaparte' was on his marriage-lines. His nomination to an important command closed the door on the Corsican period. From May onwards his mother followed his example, signing herself 'Letizia Bonaparte', which is not to say that she was ready to approve Nabulio's marriage... When he arrived at Marseilles he handed her a letter from Josephine, which he had almost certainly dictated himself:

* On the day of the coronation, as soon as he had assumed the Imperial robes, he said: 'Go and find Raguideau; get him to come here at once; I want to talk to him.' Raguideau was immediately fetched, whereupon Napoleon said: 'Have I nothing but my name and my sword?' (Bourrienne: *Mémoires*.)

'So you have become a great general,' exclaimed Madame Letizia, playing for time.*

'General-in-Chief, which isn't always the same thing.'

She did acknowledge the letter from the 'schemer', the 'intruder', but only when nine days had elapsed since she last embraced Nabulio as he hurried away to his rendezvous with history in Italy, calling to her before he threw himself into his carriage:

'Take care of your health for my sake, Mother; you must live long, for if you were to die I should have no equals left in the world.'*

Did Josephine recognise her husband's style as she read her mother-in-law's letter?

'I received your letter, Madame, which added nothing to the idea I had already formed of you. My son had told me of his happy union, and from that moment you had my approval as well as my esteem. The only thing lacking to make one happy is the satisfaction of meeting you. Be assured that I feel all a mother's tenderness for you and you are as dear to me as my own children.

'My son has encouraged me to hope that you will come to him at Marseilles, and your letter confirms this. I look forward to the pleasure your stay here will give me, Madame.

'My daughters join with me in urging you not to delay this happy occasion. Meanwhile, please believe that my children are with me in assuring you of the same fondness they feel for their brother.'

'Words, words, mere words, no matter from the heart!' Madame Letizia already entertained for this woman who had taken possession of Nabulio, body and soul, a hatred which did not cease until the divorce in 1809.

They could not have been more unlike one another – the pious, suspicious Corsican, parsimonious to the verge of avarice, whose reserve bordered on mistrust, whose sole pleasure lay in shielding and enriching her family – and the frivolous, carefree, voluble

* *Mémoires de Napoléon Bonaparte*. A collection of anecdotes published in 1834.

creole, with no regard for truth. Neither of the two came half-way to meet the other across the void that separated them.

After Nabulio, it was sixteen-year-old Pauline's turn to embark on an amorous adventure and fall in love with a man old enough to be her father, and what a man! The charming Pauline, of whom Metternich (a connoisseur in such matters) wrote that she was 'as beautiful as it is possible to be', became infatuated with Fréron, a revolutionary who had terrorised Marseilles and Toulon with his bloodthirsty reprisals, and recently been appointed Commissary of the Convention, but now, realising his star was waning, was anxious to be a hanger-on in young General Bonaparte's train. A womaniser and fine figure of a man, but cynical and debauched, rotten with syphilis ... The foolish child encouraged him with ardent letters, in the style of: 'Love me always, my soul, my own, my tender beloved; I breathe for you alone, I love you ... I love you, my beautiful idol, you are my heart, my tender beloved.' It was Diderot who wrote that love gives intelligence to those who have none, but destroys it in those who have it, or words to that effect.

Alerted by Madame Letizia, Nabulio poured cold water on this erotic delirium and simply instructed Joseph: 'I beg you to settle Paulette's affair; I do not intend her to marry Fréron; tell her so, and make her tell him.' Pauline submitted, but wept long and bitterly, and this strange adventure left her with the disease which finally destroyed her after endless agony.

At this time Italy was echoing with the sound of gunfire that secured the victories of Montenotte, Millesimo and Mondovi. On May 15, Nabulio's armies entered Milan. As Stendhal wrote, it was 'the purest and most brilliant period of his life ... No general, whether ancient or modern, had won so many battles in so short a time, with such a miserable army, and against such powerful enemies.' Marseilles, proud of its Bonapartes, organised a victory celebration, presided over by Madame Letizia and her daughters, who stood erect but moved to tears to receive the palms commemorating Nabulio's victory. As a witness wrote:

'The spectators could not restrain their emotion as they saw the laurel wreath of courage placed in the hands of virtue, grace and beauty.'

The Italian campaign brought riches to the Directory by means of Bonaparte's levies on that country, but it also led to tacit submission to the little general whose career the Directors had sponsored, and who now wrote to them recklessly: 'I am speaking for 80,000 soldiers. The time for dastardly lawyers and miserable ranters to guillotine our soldiers is past, and if you give them no choice the Italian army will arrive at the gates of Clichy with their general; but woe betide you.'

Lodi, Castiglione, Arcole, Rivoli, Tolentino, Leoben – the victories followed hot on each other's heels, but just at the moment when the Bonaparte family were surrounded by a halo of Nabulio's triumph yet another unfortunate situation involved them – the marriage of Elisa to Captain Felix Bacciochi, a big thick-featured fellow who was not remarkable either for intelligence or courage, but who was a Corsican and even came from Ajaccio. The wedding took place on May 1, 1797, a fortnight after the preliminaries of the peace of Leoben, when Bonaparte had conquered the Austrians, treated the Emperor of Austria as an equal, and announced with calm assurance to the Directory: 'I am setting up a Cisalpine republic.' As Elisa was far from attractive, thin and sour-tempered, Madame Letizia thought the marriage would do, but she lay awake wondering how she could get it accepted by Nabulio, whose success had made him touchy on the subject of alliances and other things as well. A well-timed invitation arrived from her son asking her to join him near Milan. She must take the plunge ... She packed in a daze, telling herself that the joy of reunion would help him swallow the bitter pill. But could it really?

IV
'The Mother of Bonaparte'

Madame Letizia made the journey from Marseilles to Genoa by sea, taking with her the Bacciochis, Caroline and Jerome; thence, without announcing her arrival, she set off for Milan, calmly replying to the officer who offered her an escort over the Appenines, always a risky crossing:

'No need. General Bonaparte's family have nothing to fear.'

'Bonaparte's mother' was now an affluent and elegant woman. When she saw how attentive the Genoese were to her, she may perhaps have remembered the days when they ruled Corsica, and thought how strange was the caprice of fortune by which Nabulio had now become the dreaded master of their opulent city.

The conqueror of Italy, awaiting the travellers in the luxurious Serbelloni palace in the Corso Venezia of Milan, threw himself into his mother's arms, suddenly frowned as he saw Elisa hanging on to the arm of an unknown man, and listened with a stony expression to Madame Letizia's involved explanations. He was on the verge of giving way to one of his famous paroxysms of rage, but desisted on seeing his sister's hypocritical tears; instead he made everyone get into a carriage to go to Mombello, where Josephine was waiting – Josephine, who had reached Italy by the Route des Alpes and had not yet met her mother-in-law.

The castle of Mombello, a handsome building delightfully

situated near Limbiate just north of Milan, had all the air of a royal Court, with general officers coming and going, including some whose names would soon be on every lip – Murat, Bernadotte, Junot, Berthier and Lannes; with princes, ministers, scholars and artists crowding round the young conqueror, who was preparing with calm confidence the decree establishing the Cisalpine Republic, as he had condescended to inform the Directory. One of those present, the poet Arnault, expressed his amazement: 'Nothing astonished me so much as the attitude of this small man surrounded by giants whom he was dominating by sheer character. It was not pride, but it revealed the assurance of a man who knows his own worth and feels he is in his proper place. Bonaparte had no need to stand on tiptoe to put himself on the same level as the rest, he was already spared that trouble. Not one of those he talked to seemed taller than him.' And a foreign diplomat remarked in some trepidation: 'He was no longer the general of a triumphant republic, he was a conqueror in his own right.'

Poor Madame Letizia! Everything about Josephine, reigning over her Court like an elegant and frivolous sovereign or a carefree goddess, was instantly displeasing to her: her fantastic style of dress, her coquettish ways, her lap-dog, and even the passion she inspired in Nabulio, not to mention her infatuation for a little nonentity called Captain Charles ... At the lavish dinners and concerts the contrast between the two women was striking – the one over-powdered to conceal the irreparable damage of the years, decked out in silk, gauze and pearls; the other, only thirteen or fourteen years her senior, with the charming complexion and simple dress of a plain-living countrywoman.

What passed in her for reserve was in fact her preference for silence rather than mangling a language she did not feel at home in. It was better for them both that they shouldn't stay in the same house too long.

The time came when Nabulio decided to marry Pauline to Leclerc, a brigadier-general with a handsome fortune, whom he had known since the siege of Toulon. Like Elisa, Pauline would receive a dowry of 40,000 *livres*. Madame Letizia was delighted, and on June 14, 1797 a Corsican priest blessed Pauline's union and regularised that of the Bacciochis in the chapel of San Francisco adjoining the castle of Mombello. Moreover, an old friend of hers, the worthy Captain Felix was promoted major and given the command of the Ajaccio defences, a post he took up at once, now that Corsica had been liberated.* What a happy chance for Madame Letizia, who was to sail on the same ship! Corsica, Ajaccio, the citadel, the family home. She would find it embellished by Joseph, who had been chosen by his compatriots to sit among the Five Hundred and had had time to undertake its repair during his electoral campaign, Nabulio having insisted that it must be ready for 'any emergency'.

With what a sigh of relief she left Mombello and its parties, intrigues and tittle-tattle! It was four years since Madame Letizia had left her island, reviled and pursued, and she was far from sorry to return haloed with the glory of a son who would certainly insist on apologies from all and sundry. Naturally, the town gave her a wildly enthusiastic welcome. It was the same person who stepped ashore, erect, distant and severe, as she surveyed all her new 'friends' with the cool gaze they knew so well, but Nabulio had made his way in the world and the Corsicans were not the last to be dazzled by the force that carries all before it – power.

Here was the port, the old square, the narrow streets smelling of fish and fried blackbirds, and the Casa Bonaparte itself. Used by the English troops as a store for fodder, pillaged by the Paolists, occupied for a while by a weasel-faced major called Hudson Lowe (of whom more would be heard), and incompletely repaired by Joseph, neither its wall-papers, hangings, nor curtains were recognisable. As for the familiar objects, they had all disappeared.

* Bonaparte's successes in Italy had impelled the British Viceroy, Sir Gilbert Elliot, and his supporters (among them Pozzo di Borgo) to re-embark for England, under the protection of Nelson's ships.

It was rather as if the vandals had smashed the past itself in pieces.*

With the 97,500 francs indemnity granted to Madame Letizia by the Directory as a victim of Paolist damage – the Welfare State was not born yesterday – and with the help of her dear Lucien, Commissary for War in Corsica, she set about lovingly recreating the décor of her youth, improving on it even, to show friends and enemies alike what stuff the Bonapartes were made of. Her house was to be beautiful, the most beautiful in Ajaccio, worthy of the young general of whom she wrote 'he has devoted his whole life to the well-being of all France, not only of his family'. She sent for tiles for floor and roof, and cast-iron banisters from Marseilles – Joseph's mother-in-law, Madame Clary, supervised the order and its transport, also that of two lots of wall-paper, one red and white and the other daffodil-yellow, three rolls of red paper and eight of roses on a poppy-coloured ground . . . three bells for the rooms, and a length of white linen cord for the window-curtains . . . eight chairs and an arm-chair in daffodil-yellow damask 'in the modern style'. In return for Madame Clary's kindness she was sent a sack of chestnuts from Ajaccio. Madame Letizia was not exactly mean, but she thought that being of service to General Bonaparte's mother could be reckoned an honour!

Ah, what pleasant evenings she would spend in her pretty drawing-room, sitting in her daffodil-coloured arm-chair, thinking how well settled her children were – Joseph, French Ambassador to the Holy See of all places (Joseph who had so little liking for ecclesiastical life); Pauline, with a husband in command at Milan;

* The history of the Casa Bonaparte is extremely eventful. Napoleon gave it to André Ramolino, a cousin on his mother's side; from him it went to Joseph Bonaparte and then to his daughter Zénaïde, Princess of Canino, who offered it to Napoleon III. Finally the Empress Eugénie bequeathed it to her nephew, Prince Victor, grandson of Jerome Bonaparte, who offered it to France in 1923. It is now a very well arranged National Museum where, among the exhibits, Madame Mère's beloved daffodil-yellow chairs can be seen along with a number of other things belonging to her.

'The Mother of Bonaparte'

Caroline, a pupil in a famous school kept by the former reader to Queen Marie-Antoinette. As for Louis and Jerome, they were advancing in their careers in Nabulio's shadow. But Nabulio! How well everything was going, marvellously well, if only he didn't try and do too many things at once. Hadn't he just left Paris – Paris, where reputations were made, but could also be lost – to go off to Egypt in pursuit of some glorious chimera. After he left, Josephine had returned to her irregular life, while the Directors reeled from error to error and from clumsiness to knavery, so that the future . . . Madame Letizia sighed deeply, sitting in her pretty daffodil-yellow arm-chair.

Luckily she had Fesch with her – Fesch, who was now himself a Commissary for War, Fesch who was described by Metternich (as much a connoisseur of the clergy as of pretty women) as 'a strange mixture of bigotry and ambition'. Having returned from Italy rolling in money and probably with definite notions of the importance of his mission as military purveyor, he settled into his native town with happy ostentation. He had bought two properties, for 25,000 *livres*, to house his fine collection of paintings (Italian of course), and skilfully invested his capital of 750,000 francs to advantage.

'If only it lasts,' Madame Letizia muttered once more! 'If only it lasts. . . .'

But suppose the wind should change? And wasn't it bound to change? The power of the Directory was falling to the distaff side, the Paolists of Ajaccio were beginning to hold up their heads again, and Madame Letizia read hatred and envy on more than one face – hatred of the clan who had joined the Jacobins to get on in the world, envy of the fine fortune they had speedily acquired. Worse still, there was Josephine's behaviour: while Nabulio roamed through the desert she bought herself the château of Malmaison, where she kept open house in company with that puppy Captain Charles, 'a young man with the face of a whore', who had been fluttering round her ever since Milan. All Paris gloated over General Bonaparte's 'misfortune', and one of the Directors went in person to rebuke the faithless wife. Joseph's letters were full of outrageous pieces of scandal.

Most opportunely Louis arrived; he had just been promoted Major in Egypt and was able to land in Corsica on his way to take the trophies of the new campaign to the Directory, after a journey complicated by bad weather and the English navy. It was now December 1798, and Madame Letizia was making a slow and unsatisfactory recovery from an attack of malaria which had kept her in bed for a month; the sight of her son, the stories he brought of Nabulio's new brilliant successes gave her pleasure, but what made her tremble with joy was his account of the fury of the deceived husband when informed of Josephine's escapades. Louis assured her that he had been heard to shout:

'Unfaithful to me – that woman! . . . Curses on them all . . . I'll exterminate the whole lot of her puppies and fops . . . As for her, it's divorce!'*

Did Madame Letizia tell herself that Nabulio might need her? Did she give in to the entreaties of Louis, who believed that she was in danger in a country on the brink of a fresh revolt? We do not know, but at the beginning of 1799 she and her son set sail, and by March she was in Paris installed in one floor of the fine house recently bought by Joseph in the rue du Rocher.

* * *

The days when the Bonaparte family lived on support from the Convention seemed very far away now! When Joseph left his house in Paris, it was to play at living like a lord at Mortefontaine, an estate of 600 hectares of woods, fields, nursery-garden and ornamental lakes, which he had bought for the tidy sum of 258,000 francs, and was beautifying with grottoes, water-nymphs, an orangery and a theatre. Everyone who had made a name for himself in politics and literature visited him there.

Lucien had a seat among the Five Hundred and already domi-

* Bourrienne: *Mémoires*.

'The Mother of Bonaparte'

nated the Assembly by his passionate and gifted oratory; when he was preparing an important speech he used to retreat to Plessis-Chamant, a handsome estate near Senlis. Pauline and General Leclerc owned Montgobert, in the Aisne, and Désirée Clary, Joseph's sister-in-law, was marrying Bernadotte, at present only a general, but who would soon be a marshal and King of Sweden.

On October 13, 1799 the news broke that Bonaparte had disembarked at Fréjus, was marching towards Paris, where he was expected at any moment, was in fact arriving, and the Directors trembled in their shoes, because the young military leader was as popular as they were detested. Joseph, Lucien, Louis and Leclerc galloped to meet him – anxious to get there before Josephine, who was approaching through Burgundy – they told him that power was ready to drop into his hands like a ripe fruit, and that his wife was unworthy of him and should be repudiated. Meanwhile the crowds massed along his route and shouted 'Long live Bonaparte!'

At dawn on the 16th the Man of Destiny arrived in his house in the rue des Victoires and found it empty; in the course of the morning Madame Letizia was announced and was embraced by a tearful Nabulio, who refused to go and stay with Joseph in the rue du Rocher, however ... And two days later, just before midnight (for she had made careful calculations) Josephine arrived, after having driven as far as Lyons when she heard her husband was already home. She collapsed in front of the door of his room, knocked, wept, sobbed and implored, swore to repent; brought her two children, Eugène and Hortense, to add their tears, sobs and entreaties to her own – and won the day. Next morning, when Lucien arrived, he found her in bed with Nabulio, smiling, even triumphant. If Nabulio had only followed his mother's advice, and moved to the rue du Rocher, the 'schemer' would have been defeated. The only consolation for Madame Letizia was to hear that Nabulio sometimes confided to his friends:

'The soldiers of the Egyptian campaign are much like those at the Siege of Troy, and their wives are about as faithful.'

Three weeks later the *coup d'état* of Brumaire 18 saw the triumph of the three Bonaparte brothers. Madame Letizia had been informed of the plot to overthrow the Directory... yet she passed an anxious day.

'She was calm, but very uneasy,' Madame d'Abrantès records, 'her extreme pallor and the convulsive start she gave every time she heard an unexpected sound, was almost painful to see. It was now that I formed a very high opinion of her... The fates of three of her sons were being decided; one of them could have been struck down, even if the other two escaped. She felt this, and felt it deeply.'

Lucien kept sending his valet to her, to reassure her; and when, at this critical moment on the 19th, a woman visitor expressed surprise at not seeing her with Josephine, she replied curtly: 'That's not where I should choose to go to find peace of mind.'

The Legislative Assembly, terrified by false rumours, had taken refuge at St. Cloud, where Nabulio and Lucien were failing to settle their business quite as briskly as they had hoped: the former, jostled by excited members of parliament, owed his safety to the latter, who saved the situation with the help of the grenadiers, when Murat cheerfully ordered them:

'Send this whole lot packing!'

Later that day, a few bewildered deputies trembling with fear were rounded up in the park, and made to vote for the document which replaced the Directory by the Consulate. That evening, perhaps so as to put people off the scent, Madame Letizia and Pauline had dined with an old friend called Madame Permon, and at seven o'clock the ladies had gone calmly off to the theatre.* However, Madame Letizia seemed uneasy. Paris certainly looked calm enough under the rain, but what was happening at St. Cloud? During the interval an uproar suddenly broke out in the

---

* It was in Madame Permon's house at Montpellier that Carlo Bonaparte had died. Her daughter Laure married General Junot, Duc d'Abrantès, and left some famous *Mémoires*.

'The Mother of Bonaparte'

pit, where a thief had just been arrested, and she started, and turned rather white. The play went on again, and then all of a sudden the actors were interrupted by an individual who came on to the stage and announced:

'Citizens, General Bonaparte has narrowly escaped being assassinated at St. Cloud, by traitors to our Country.'

The rumour was based on the fact that Nabulio had been taken aside by some deputies who threatened to outlaw him.

The women left in great haste, Pauline uttering shrill cries but Madame Letizia in control of herself. They hurried to the rue des Victoires and were relieved to learn that Nabulio had been nominated Consul, in fact First Consul of the Republic.

'One never climbs so high as when one has no idea where one is going,' Napoleon was to say one day.

* * *

The Consulate was a period of reforms carried out with drums beating, a turning-point in the history of France, a time of social change. It also witnessed the prodigious rise of all the Bonapartes: Lucien was made Minister of the Interior at twenty-four years old; Joseph Councillor of State and member of the Legislative Assembly; Louis – at twenty – commanded a regiment of dragoons. The Constitution of the year VIII gave Nabulio powers as extensive as a king's based on divine right; when it was approved the First Consul and Josephine moved into the Tuileries, and Madame Letizia was offered the Palace of the Luxembourg, built for Marie de Medicis. She refused it point-blank. Would she prefer rooms in the palace of the Tuileries? Again she refused, and went to live with her brother, who had just bought a house in the rue du Mont-Blanc, in two drawing-rooms and a few bedrooms. On January 18, 1800, Caroline had married Murat, the handsome cavalry officer of whom Nabulio – who didn't care for him – used often to say: 'I quite agree ... he was superb at Aboukir.' Jerome lived at the Tuileries in his brother's shadow; Letizia was free to go where she liked. She was often seen at Mortefontaine or Plessis-Chamant, but rarely at Malmaison, where she made it a point of honour – or perhaps of malice – always to appear very simply dressed, to draw attention to Josephine's crazy finery.

'We were in the country,' said one of Josephine's ladies-in-waiting: 'Madame Bonaparte, the Consul's mother, seemed to us a quite unpretentious woman. She had only brought one cotton dress with her; Madame Leclerc, her daughter, teased her about it. "Be quiet you extravagant girl," her mother said to her. "I have to think of putting something by for your brothers; they aren't all established yet. You only think of youthful pleasures at your age, but at mine I'm concerned with security. I don't want Bonaparte to complain, you take too much advantage of his good-nature."'

Relations between mother-in-law and daughter-in-law went from bad to worse, and a scene took place at Mortefontaine which frightened all the guests: just as they were going in to dinner, Joseph offered his mother his arm to take her to the place of honour next to him. This didn't suit the First Consul, Chief of State, and he frowned, decided to play the part of master of the house himself, and told Josephine – the 'intruder' – to sit beside him. On another occasion Madame Letizia was the aggressor: when she heard that Fouché, who was Minister of Police and very thick with Josephine, was allowing the newspapers to confirm the rumour that Lucien was incapable of running his Ministry, she hurried to the Tuileries. Josephine happened to be in Nabulio's study ... The *Madre* raised her voice, the wife wept. Nabulio strode up and down the room.

'Kindly warn your friend Fouché,' Madame Letizia told her daughter-in-law, 'that I think my arms are long enough to make anyone who slanders my son regret it, whoever he may be.'

Alas, there is no smoke without fire, and soon after this Nabulio himself began to be suspicious of Lucien's behaviour. The Minister of the Interior, closely in touch with Bernadotte – who was intriguing against the First Consul – was also mixed up in shady transactions concerning the income from octroi and supplies: this sort of thing couldn't possibly be acceptable to the man who had declared war on corruption.* Lucien was obliged to resign, and to separate him from temptation and his disturbing friends Nabulio appointed him ambassador to the court of Madrid, with the special mission of preparing the peace treaties with Spain and Portugal. More of a demagogue than a democrat, a man of brilliant but erratic intelligence, Lucien went from blunder to blunder, innocently and cheerfully excusing his behaviour by explaining that he would put an end to wars between France and these two countries.

This first disgrace of the son whom she may have secretly loved a little more than the rest, saddened Madame Letizia. 'Your attitude makes me unhappy,' she wrote to Madrid, 'I console myself by thinking of your return and of the moment when I have the satisfaction of folding you in my arms ... you can imagine how uneasy I feel at having all my family scattered; I won't say anything more.'

A second shadow, and a considerable one, was cast on the happiness of the clan by the attempted assassination of December 1800, in the rue St. Nicaise, organised by the Chouans (royalists of the West) with English support. The instability of a regime depending on a single man was apparent to all, and there began to be talk of a Consulate for life and of the choice of his successor by the First Consul himself, a decision which all the Bonapartes awaited with calm confidence, so natural did it seem to them that the glory won by Nabulio should remain in the family. The agitation felt by Madame Letizia after this terrifying assassination attempt, costing a dozen lives and from which Nabulio only escaped by a miracle, was soothed in July 1801 when a Concordat

* It seems that Lucien was dreaming of a duumvirate, giving the civil power to him and the military power to Bernadotte. Bonaparte got wind of this threat, and warned Bernadotte that if he persisted in his plans 'he would have him shot on the Place du Carrousel'.

was signed rallying all the French Catholics to the First Consul; they repeated his words:

'A society without religion is like a ship without a compass.'

Roman Catholicism was hereby recognised as the religion of the great majority of French people, and freedom of worship was restored. The First Consul had indeed patiently nibbled away Papal pretensions and turned the document in his favour, by adding the 'organic clauses' by which the clergy were made functionaries of the State, but the devout Madame Letizia rejoiced above all that God had returned to France and its homes.

Unfortunately, with Nabulio, cold always followed heat, and now he took it into his head to marry his brother Louis to Hortense, Josephine's daughter. As Lucien wrote in his Memoirs, 'Our mother was obviously much annoyed by this union. She saw in it the triumph of a family alien to her own.' At St. Helena, Napoleon was to say of this marriage:

'It was the result of Josephine's intriguing for her own ends.'

Did the beautiful creole, who could no longer give the ruler of France a child, really believe she could avoid the threat of divorce by tightening the links between her family and the Bonapartes? Probably, but poor Hortense made a very bad bargain when she accepted this young man, who – though once charming – became unstable, melancholic, suspicious and touchy as his health deteriorated. Some said that falls from his horse had damaged his spinal marrow; others more cynically, enumerated the affairs with women which had left their painful aftermath. The bride couldn't conceal her tears on her wedding-day, and Madame Letizia was sullen and gloomy, even when the Pope's legate honoured Murat and Caroline by regularising their marriage afterwards.

As was to be expected, once the Concordat was signed the First Consul remembered he had an ecclesiastic in the family – his uncle Fesch, the former Abbé Fesch – and appointed him Archbishop of Lyons, at the same time asking the Pope to bestow a cardinal's hat upon him. So here was Madame Letizia's brother an eminence and Primate of the Gauls, and soon afterwards ambassador to the Holy See, with the writer–diplomat Chateaubriand as his secretary.

At the end of 1802 General Leclerc died at Santo Domingo, and Pauline, who had gone with him on this campaign, returned to Paris in tears, which didn't prevent her from casting eyes at Prince Camillo Borghese, an extremely handsome young man – too handsome said the gossips – possessing one of the noblest names in Italy, a fortune of two millions and countless palaces. She married him ten months later, thus becoming the first princess in the family.

As in the story-books, the good fairies do not always have the last word: a sudden quarrel flared up between Nabulio and *caro Luciano*, who left his fine embassy in Madrid in November 1802 on his own initiative, after writing to the First Consul, who had reprimanded him for his bad treaty with Spain and Portugal: 'I don't deny that I lack many qualities; I've known for a long time that I'm too young for public affairs, and I therefore want to retire, and make good my deficiencies.' Four days later he was in Paris, and his wife Christine having died eighteen months earlier, he formed a connexion with a ravishing Spanish lady, the Marquesa de Santa Cruz. On the eve of his departure the King of Spain sent him his portrait and five millions in diamonds, but rumour with its usual malignancy was not slow to disclose that his trunks also contained some fifty millions, twenty masterpieces of painting and two hundred thousand crowns worth of precious stones.* Provided with this impressive fortune he bought the magnificent Hôtel de Brienne in the Faubourg Saint-Germain, sold his stones at Amsterdam and invested money in London, Rome and the United States, afterwards holding a sort of court, where (to the First Consul's fury) he invited all republicans who were opposed to the regime. On May 24, 1803, a child was born,

* These figures are quoted by Madame d'Abrantès, but were considered to be exaggerated by François Pietri, historian of this part of Lucien Bonaparte's life. He fixed Lucien's capital at about seven millions.

named Jules-Laurent-Lucien, whose mother he married in October. She was the widow of a stock-broker, Jouberthon, a woman of easy virtue, fond of eccentric and conspicuous finery.* He had chosen his time well! Nabulio, now that he was Consul for life, had the right to choose his successor and also to confirm the marriages of his relations. He had conceived the plan of marrying Lucien to Marie-Louise, Queen of Etruria, a short-lived kingdom in the Italian peninsula forming a part of his 'system', and since she was the daughter of Carlos IV of Spain he thought this hasty marriage extremely inconvenient from every point of view, and even 'very immoral'. Madame Letizia at once took the side of the child she considered was having the worst of it.

'The Consul knows very well that he has no right to insist on your marrying to please him, any more than his own marriage pleased you, or indeed me.'†

Corsican bitterness is long-lived... To show her disapproval she received the new wife with due ceremony, and accepted from her *caro Luciano*, who was now so rich, an annuity of twenty-four thousand francs. Nabulio stifled his anger and tried persuasion; he made his rebellious brother a senator, a Grand Officer of the Order of the Legion of Honour and a member of the Institute of France. All to no avail! Their meetings were stormy, as Nabulio had the effrontery to suggest openly that 'the hussy' should be divorced. Lucien replied curtly to Joseph, who sometimes played the part of go-between:

'My wife, my son, my daughter and I are as one.'

In the utmost distress, Madame Letizia witnessed this family quarrel which upset the whole clan and became a civil war, with the two brothers as enemies. In February 1804 the problem of an heir to the First Consul (who would soon be Emperor), was of prime

---

* When Napoleon reproached him for marrying 'a loose woman', and a '*merveilleuse*' Lucien cracked back at him with 'At least mine is young and pretty'. A savage allusion to Josephine, who had once been both – but many years earlier...

† Lucien Bonaparte: *Mémoires*.

Joseph Bonaparte,
King of Spain, 1768–1844

Napoleon

Lucien Bonaparte,
Prince of Canino, 1775–1840

Elisa Bacciochi,
Princess de Lucques et de Piombino,
1777–1820

Louis Bonaparte,
King of Holland, 1778–1846

Pauline Borghèse,
Duchesse de Guastalla, 1780–1825

Caroline Murat,
Queen of Naples, 1782–1839

Jerome Bonaparte,
King of Westphalia, 1784–1860

'The Mother of Bonaparte'

importance to Joseph and Louis, and kept Lucien in Paris for a while. At the beginning of April he was summoned to St. Cloud, for a frank explanation which led to a definite breach, and as he left the meeting Napoleon explained to Josephine:

'Well, that's the end! I've just broken with Lucien and sent him away.'

This happened only a month before the proclamation of the Empire, so that the ambitious but illogical Lucien was shutting the door on a succession to which he vaguely believed he had a right, and that for love – 'that folly committed by two people', as Nabulio sometimes called it.

A few days later the coaches of the Senator brother of the First Consul waited, fully laden, in the courtyard of the Hôtel de Brienne. On the first floor, Lucien and Joseph were walking up and down and talking, while Madame Letizia and Alexandrine Jouberthon sat on a sofa conversing in subdued tones. As a last hope they were waiting for a message from the Tuileries, some sign of reconciliation, or even pardon.

'Well, my sons,' said the *Madre*, 'the time has come for you to part.'

'No, not yet, mother,' murmured Joseph. 'Lucien has just promised me to wait till midnight. I still hope that *he* will recall him.'

'Napoleon won't recall your brother,' said Madame Letizia shortly. 'He doesn't want to have him anywhere near him.'

'Why shouldn't he want him? If Lucien doesn't interfere with him, our brother isn't unfriendly.'

Lucien interrupted innocently: 'But I've never interfered with him, except in my ministerial capacity.'

'It's only half past eleven, Mother. The Consul doesn't go to bed before midnight,' said Joseph. 'Supposing I went back ... supposing I asked him to give me another letter for Lucien, telling him not to go away?'

'Yes,' said Madame Letizia forcefully, 'a fine thing for you, his eldest brother to go and beg him to let Lucien stay, so that he can reply angrily, as he did to me and even to Josephine: "Anyone who is so upset at seeing him go can go with him!"'

Joseph suggested that Lucien should go himself and beg 'forgiveness'.

'Ought I to go?' Lucien asked his mother.

'No, my son, you ought not. And besides it would be quite useless. I remember what he said to me in his rage.'

'If that's all,' said Lucien lightly, 'I'm not afraid of his rages.'

'That's fine,' the *Madre* said quietly, 'but you're both of you hot-tempered. Napoleon is all-powerful. I would much prefer you to leave without seeing him.'*

The marble clock struck midnight. Lucien and his family jumped into their coaches and set off on their way to Italy.

A few days later the First Consul exclaimed: 'How can I reform the morals of the country, when a woman like that is brought into my family? The French people are a moral race. Their rulers should be the same. Anyone who isn't with me is against me. I have duties. I will carry them out.'

The glorious year of 1804, the year that saw the restoration of the ancient imperial dignity, was not a happy one for Madame Letizia. At the very moment when Nabulio and Luciano were confronting each other like two Corsican moufflons, the news broke that the Duc d'Enghien, cousin of the Bourbons, had been executed, horrifying both Madame Letizia and Josephine. It was essentially a political move, costing the life of a young prince who was frivolous rather than guilty, and it shattered the hopes of royalist France. England had declared war on France in 1803, and given large subsidies to the royalists of the Vendée, who were hatching a plot to destroy the First Consul. When their leaders, Moreau, Pichegru and Cadoudal were arrested they revealed that if their coup had succeeded a French prince would have arrived in Paris.

'Am I a dog to be struck down in the street,' cried Bonaparte,

* Lucien Bonaparte: *Mémoires*.

'The Mother of Bonaparte'

'while my murderers are treated as sacred? They are attacking my life. I shall return war with war.'

On the advice of Talleyrand and Fouché, he gave orders for the duke to be arrested on foreign territory close to the frontier; he was condemned to death as an exile in the pay of the enemy, and shot at dawn on March 20.* If Paris remained calm, unaware of this hasty justice, Malmaison was living through a sort of nightmare, and for once all the women of the family sided with Josephine, who sobbed:

'I'm only a woman. I admit that this event moves me to tears.'

'My mother was in floods of tears,' wrote Joseph. 'She reproached the First Consul bitterly and he listened in silence. She told him it was an atrocious act, of which nothing could ever cleanse him, and that he had given in to the treacherous advice of his own enemies, who were delighted to be able to sully the history of his life with such a horrible page.' We know now that Madame Letizia was mistaken. When he was making his Will on St. Helena Napoleon wrote with a firm hand: 'I had the Duc d'Enghien arrested and tried because it became necessary for the safety, interest and honour of the French people when the Comte d'Artois admitted to having sixty assassins in Paris. In similar circumstances I would do the same again.' All she could do was to arrange that 'a lady' named by the prince before he died, and who was almost certainly his wife, the Princess de Rohan-Chabot, should receive certain objects that were on his person, as well as his dog Mohilow, who was terrified by witnessing his master's execution and was taken from the freshly filled grave at dawn by a tender-hearted gardener.

* * *

* In the course of his interrogation the duke is said to have declared: 'I am still in the pay of the English, from whom I received one hundred and fifty-five pounds a month... Hearing that war had been declared against France, I asked to serve in the English army. The government replied that that was impossible, but that I should remain on the Rhine, where I should very soon have a part to to play.'

In the hope of keeping most of his family on his side, Nabulio loaded his mother with attentions, granted her a pension of 120,000 francs and ordered a full-length portrait of her from Gérard, but all in vain.

'The child of mine I love most will always be the one who is most unfortunate,' she said shortly.

And her journey to Rome was not taken on a sudden impulse as some have believed and written: it must have been planned for several months, for in January 1804 she wrote to a French prelate:* 'It's been decided that in the spring I shall go to Italy, where I hope to regain my health and spend several pleasant months in that beautiful climate, and in the company of my brother and my beloved daughter.' No, it was not an impulse, but she was not displeased when her departure was taken as showing approval of Lucien. She travelled by short stages with her 'Household': a lady-in-waiting, a private secretary, a doctor and two lady's-maids, and was welcomed in Italy like royalty.

'Your mother has arrived in Rome,' wrote Cardinal Fesch to Nabulio ... 'She was received in the Papal States with the highest honours. At Loretto she spent the night in the papal palace. On her arrival in Rome, His Holiness ordered that a tribune should be erected for her in St. Peter's for Easter Mass, equal in importance to those of the Queen of Sardinia and the Princess of Mecklenburg; but as this stall could only be set up behind those of the above persons, who had possessed theirs for more than a year, she thought best to refuse, pleading fatigue after her journey. Yesterday I presented her to the Pope at the Quirinal, and her daughter accompanied her ... The Pope spoke to her of his regard for you, and of his prayers for your safety; he told her that he would be delighted to see her often and she should stay in his States as long as she wished. In fact she had to be the one to bring their long conversation to an end.'

Dismiss the Holy Father herself! Nabulio had certainly come a long way.

* Monseigneur d'Isoard.

'The Mother of Bonaparte'

'The Roman nobility came to call on her without waiting for her "reception" days,' the Cardinal went on: 'The Dean of the College of Cardinals invited all the cardinals to go and pay their respects to her within twenty-four hours. All of them – even the Neapolitans – hastened to pay her this honour, usually reserved for sovereigns only.'

For sovereigns! Madame Letizia suddenly realised that Nabulio was even more powerful than she had dared believe. So powerful that the Holy Father sat at his table and wrote to the First Consul: 'We cannot tell you what satisfaction we got from our interview with her. We found her worthy to be your mother.' Treating the head of the Christian Church as an equal, Nabulio replied amiably: 'I thank Your Holiness for the kind things you have said about my mother's arrival in Rome. The climate of Paris is too cold and damp for her. My chief doctor advised her to settle in a warm country, more similar to her native land. Whatever she decides to do, I shall continue to commend her to Your Holiness.'

The climate of Paris ... The advice of his chief doctor ... Nabulio was certainly a very subtle diplomat, and in four lines he annihilated the rumours about his mother's hasty departure from Paris, following so close on Lucien's.

The illustrious visitor stayed with her brother at the Falconieri Palace, and it was here that she received news of the proclamation of the Empire, unanimously voted by the Senate on May 10, 1804.

'I accept the title you believe will contribute to the glory of the Nation,' Nabulio had declared calmly.

Joseph and Louis had become Princes, Mesdames Murat and Bacciochi Imperial Highnesses. Everyone spoke of the Lord High Chamberlain, the Master of the Horse, the Grand Elector and the Grand Marshal, and it all seemed quite natural.

'Even if I married the Madonna, I shouldn't succeed in surprising the Parisians,' Nabulio had said banteringly.

Madame Letizia couldn't believe her ears. All these princes and highnesses, and Josephine Empress and Her Majesty, yet not a single word about Nabulio's mother ... All these great changes had been planned and carried out without the Emperor telling his *Madre*, without his so much as sending her a line. It was Fesch who wrote a letter of fretful protest:

'Sire,

'In spite of all Your Imperial Majesty's pre-occupations, I believe it to be my duty to refer briefly to your mother and her position.

'Your mother has gone to take the waters at Lucca. Her health has been affected by moral rather than by physical ailments. I have noticed that she felt worse every time she saw the courier arrive without any letters for her. Learning of the proclamation of the Empire through the gazettes has greatly distressed her. She has been very upset not to receive any special communication during her three months in Rome. She feels that Your Imperial Majesty has put every other member of the family before herself. These disturbing thoughts are undermining her strong constitution, and undoing all the good she should have derived from her journey, the climate and her treatment. I have done all I can for her, I have neglected nothing that might calm her and make her stay in Rome pleasant...

'Your mother aspires to a title, a settled position. She is upset by being called "Your Majesty" or "Empress Mother" by some, while others merely address her as "Imperial Highness", like her daughters. She is impatient to hear what has been decided. She does not wish to return to Rome, but hopes Your Imperial Majesty will send for her to Paris before the end of August, when she is due to leave Lucca.'

Wiles such as a village priest might employ: to accuse Nabulio of undermining his mother's health, of destroying the saintly woman by inches! Perhaps the Cardinal would have profited from the new Emperor's acid comment, when opposing his sister's requests for titles and honours:

'To hear them talk, anyone might think I'd defrauded my family of their inheritance from the late king, our father.'

'The Mother of Bonaparte'

Then suddenly rumours were heard, followed by the bombshell that the Pope himself, Pius VII, was to renew the Carolingian tradition by going to Paris in person in December, 'to give a religious character to the ceremony of the anointing and coronation of the first Emperor of the French'. And at the same time Nabulio sent to ask his mother to hasten her return to Paris, but without even mentioning the question of rank and title. The monster! The *Madre* relapsed into sulks and delayed her preparations. On November she was still at Rome. When she did at last set off she made a first stop with Lucien whose wife had given birth to a daughter christened Letizia, and didn't arrive in Paris – still out of temper – until the evening of December 19. Nabulio's head had been encircled by the imperial crown more than a fortnight earlier.

V

'Her Imperial Highness, Madame, Mother of His Majesty the Emperor'

The ostentatious display with which this Empire was taking shape before her eyes was bitter to Madame Letizia. Nabulio – whom she must now call 'the Emperor' like everyone else – treated her coldly, and it was she who had to make the first move, bored by the deserted drawing-rooms of the Hôtel de Brienne, which she had bought from Lucien.

The occasion was provided by Jerome, the unruly Benjamin of the family, of whom the learned Chaptal, a man of upright judgement if ever there was one, wrote later: 'It would be difficult to find a vainer, worse brought up, more ignorant and ambitious young man.' Given the command of the frigate *Épervier* at the age of sixteen, with the mission of cruising in the West Indies, he preferred to go to the United States where he became enamoured of a certain Elizabeth Patterson, whom he married in December 1803, without asking permission of his mother or the First Consul. And that at nineteen, in other words a minor, disqualified from marrying without parental consent. 'I am waiting for a chance to introduce my beloved wife to you,' this impetuous son wrote to his mother, just at the time of the drama caused by his brother Lucien's marriage to Madame Jouberthon.

But clouds were gathering overhead: the French Ambassador to the United States received orders to pay him no more subsidies, and the captains of French merchant ships not on any pretext to take on board 'the young woman with whom citizen Jerome is involved'. A few months later, when the Empire was proclaimed, Jerome was quite simply excluded from the succession, like Lucien. Poor Madame Letizia, tired of being sent to Coventry in marble halls, brought herself peace of mind on February 22, 1805, at the cost of a solemn maternal declaration before a notary, against the marriage contracted by her son (a minor) in a foreign country – a document dictated by Nabulio who declared bleakly:

'My family is a political one.'*

How could she resist, even feebly, this terrible 'whirlwind' of a child who had become an omnipresent and omnipotent sovereign; and besides, how dare she believe he wasn't right, when the Church, the Chiefs of State, all those holding worldly power, praised his lucidity, his intelligence and his foresight; when the Archbishop of Paris declared in a pastoral letter: 'He is the man standing on the right hand of God,' and the Bishop of Amiens went further still with: 'The All-Powerful, having created Napoleon, rested from his labours.'

Ah how difficult it was to be Nabulio's mother! So Madame Letizia gave in, and made herself persuade Lucien to do likewise, not without cause, for there was a question concerning the Kingdom of Italy, which Joseph had never wanted and which Nabulio had reserved for himself by putting it under the administration of a viceroy. Viceroy of Italy? That would suit Lucien,

---

* When Jerome gave in, his marriage was annulled and he was married to the daughter of the King of Würtemberg, by the decision of his brother, who wrote to him, as to a defeated enemy: 'There is no fault that can't be erased by true repentance, in my view. Your union with Miss Patterson is null and void in the eyes of both religion and the law. Write to tell Miss Patterson to return to the United States. I will allow her 60,000 francs annuity for life, on condition that she will in no circumstances use my name. You must make her understand that you could not and will not be able to change the situation. When your marriage is thus annulled by your own wish, I will restore my friendship, and return to the feelings I have had for you since childhood, hoping that you will make yourself worthy of them by your determination to win my gratitude and distinguish yourself in my armies.'

caro Luciano. Seduced by the idea, Lucien made the first move as soon as he was informed that the Emperor was due to arrive at Milan, where his coronation would take place on May 26.

'I hasten to inform Your Majesty of my departure for Pesaro, whither I will take with me the same feelings of unalterable devotion, proof against all the vexations that pursue me,' he wrote to his brother. 'Any sign of your goodwill, Sire, would be very precious, for although circumstances have excluded me from the political family of French princes, I do not feel I have deserved, and beg you to spare me, expressions of your hatred.'

Madame Letizia soon found out Nabulio's reaction to this letter:

'On the eve of his departure we had a conversation about you, and I was completely satisfied by the goodwill he showed towards you,' she wrote to Lucien. 'The hope of a forthcoming reconciliation between my children is balm and consolation to my heart. You know there will be no peace for me until I have brought it about, but I need your help for that. You have always given me proofs of your respect; now is the time to give me the greatest of all. Campi will write and tell you what must be done; follow his instructions. Your mother begs it of you.* It's not enough to make a start, the task must be completed. Take advantage of this favourable moment; don't let slip this excellent chance of becoming reunited with your brother, and so making yourself, your family, and me happy.'

Joseph, more accurately than his mother, threw a shadow on the picture by mentioning to Lucien that the Emperor had added:

'As for his wife, I will not see her, but if Lucien satisfies my expectations I will do everything for him consistent with my firm resolve never to recognise his wife as my sister-in-law. But Lucien

---

* Campi, Lucien Bonaparte's friend, who had been his secretary-general and factotum both at the Ministry of the Interior and the French embassy at Madrid. 'An intelligent and excellent man, a republican of the old school. . . . He drank nothing but water and never ate meat.' (Madame d'Abrantès.)

'Her Imperial Highness'

has intelligence: let him use it to make the best of the situation he has got himself into. That accepted, I want to do everything he may ask me.'

More ambiguity, and Lucien – bitterly wounded and furious – wrote his brother a stiff letter: 'I cannot conceal from Your Majesty the fact that until today I had not given up hope that in the end you would restore your favours to me and also to my wife and children. Your increasing prosperity, and the return of our mother to Paris have recently served to redouble my hopes. The letter I have just received from Prince Joseph destroys this illusion. He tells me that your Majesty will do everything for me consistent with your firm resolve not to recognise my wife. This resolve, Sire, wounds me deeply, because it excludes me for ever from the public career in which I had hoped Your Majesty would honorably install me. Indeed, Sire, any distinction that emphasised the disfavour which weighs upon my dearest half, would degrade me in my own eyes; a title that could not be shared with the mother of my children would be a baleful gift and would poison the rest of my days.'

The reply came from Talleyrand, under instructions from the Emperor, and offered him a last chance:

'The Emperor grants you the freedom to return and take the place at his side to which you are entitled; but as to the conditions on which he insists, I believe his decision to be irrevocable. He wants you to agree with Madame Jouberthon to annul the contract binding you to her. He does not demand of you the sacrifice of the attachment you feel for her; he permits you to bring her to France, even to continue your present relations with her, subject only to the reserve and decency your rank ordains. He does not oppose your recognising the two children you have had by Madame Jouberthon as your natural offspring, and it will be easy for you to provide for their existence and even their happiness, for the Emperor will give you the means. His desire is to be generous to you. There are no honours or favours you cannot obtain from him.'

There followed a correspondence between Lucien, Fesch and Talleyrand, which irritated the Emperor – a man of rapid and realistic decisions – and plunged him in suppressed anger, because it was after all a question of the organisation of one of the finest kingdoms of Europe. On May 25 the blow fell: 'You have until Thursday next to reflect. On Sunday June 2, Whitsun, a decision will be made.'

The time of respite passed, and Eugène de Beauharnais was chosen, created Viceroy of Italy, and vowed fidelity to the King and Constitution on his knees in front of Napoleon, whose only comment concerning Lucien was:

'I don't want to hear any more about that affair.'

So Madame Letizia had failed with Lucien, but succeeded with Jerome: the one compensated for the other. What counted was that she had publicly played a part, for it was this that earned her what she so passionately desired. On March 23, 1805, it was officially announced that she should hold the title of 'Son Altesse Impériale, Madame, Mère de sa Majesté l'Empereur', and that her arms should be azure, a golden eagle holding in its talons a thunderbolt of the same, the thunderbolt carrying an escutcheon argent, the imperial crown being supported by semi-circles, not by eagles like that of Josephine. Her livery was the same as the Emperor's, but she could only have six horses, without page or escort. Finally she was to have a Household, and what a Household! Her Chamberlain was a duke, of Cossé-Brissac, formerly gentleman-in-waiting to the son of Louis XVI, her first equerry was General de la Bonninière de Beaumont, formerly principal page to Louis XVI, and her private secretary, Guieu, was created Baron for the occasion. Her chief almoner was the Bishop of Vercelli, assisted by two chaplains. Her ladies-in-waiting were the Baronne de Fontanges, Mesdames Davout and Soult, wives of marshals, Madame Junot, wife of the general of the Hussars, Mesdames de Saint-Pern and de Fleurieu (wife of Louis XVI's Minister for the Navy), Mesdames de Bressieux, de Laborde-Mériville, de Saint-Saveur and de Rochefort d'Ailly.

Her reader was Mademoiselle de Launay. Corvisart, doctor to the Emperor, was to be her physician-in-chief; Doctors Bourdier, Héreau, Bacher, and Désormaux were to be physicians and surgeons-in-ordinary. Saveria, the maid from Ajaccio who had seen Nabulio born and given him more than one spanking, was the only link with the past, and profited by turning herself into a power behind the throne: Madame Mère's place was on the Emperor's right, before the princes, Josephine taking the left, before the princesses. Her allowance was raised from 180,000 to 300,000 francs. This was a happy inspiration; as for the rest...

'What good is all this useless expense?' she grumbled. 'I don't need anyone to be in attendance on me, and what shall I do with chamberlains and equerries?'

A few days later, on March 26, 1805, she made her first public appearance in all her new splendour, at the chapel of the Château of St. Cloud, where Cardinal Fesch – in the august presence of the Pope – baptised the second son of Louis and Hortense, with Madame Mère as godmother and the Emperor as godfather. A very important event, as it was the first ceremony under the Empire, and a notification of the birth of 'a son to Princess Louis, the Emperor's sister-in-law', had been sent to all the Courts of Europe. The Emperor of Germany, the Pope, the Kings of Prussia, the Two Sicilies and Denmark, the Prince Regent of Portugal, the Electors of Salzburg, Bavaria, Baden, Hesse and Würtemberg had been invited, and the display was more lavish than anything dreamed of by Louis XIV... A cortège to go to the Pope in his apartments and conduct him to the chapel. A cortège to fetch the Emperor and Madame Mère and bring them to the child, which lay on a red velvet cloak edged with ermine, thrown over a bed. A procession to go to the chapel: the princes of the Empire, the princes and princesses of the Imperial family with their officers, the Empress' Household, Josephine herself surrounded by her ladies and dressed in a long ceremonial cloak held up by pages, the ministers and grand officers of the Crown, the heralds, equerries, chamberlains and then the baby in the arms of its nurse, still wrapped in the gorgeous cloak whose corners were held by four wives of marshals, and finally the Emperor, holding Madame Mère by the hand – or, as they would say at Ajaccio, *Nabulio* and his *Madre*.

In the chapel, as Madame Mère was pleased to notice, only the godparents were entitled to arm-chairs and praying-stools, Josephine having to be content with an arm-chair alone, and the princes and princesses a chair each. After the baptism there was a banquet, and then in the brilliantly lit orangery a performance of *Athalie* was given, and to finish the evening their Imperial Majesties held a reception, while outside in the park (which was open to the public) orchestras accompanied a firework display.

'My family is a political one.'

The words must have echoed in Madame Mère's ears, as she realised that Nabulio had just been emphasising his rights as head of the family in the most striking manner, by making use of all the ostentatious display the court could provide in honour of a child who was merely the fourth in the order of succession, but who had the reflected glory of bearing his name and being among his heirs.

Next the Emperor left for Italy, where in the noble cathedral of Milan he was to go to the altar and be crowned with the crown of the Lombard kings – pondering his plans for invading England the while. But Madame Mère calmly proceeded to organise her new existence, and tried to establish a timetable to occupy all these strange people revolving round her house. Let us approach on tiptoe, raise the heavy velvet door-curtain, peep into the glistening blue drawing-room and observe the scene as it was seen by Laure Junot, Duchesse d'Abrantès.

Madame Mère is now in her fifties, in other words still in her prime. In her youth she had been a great beauty as her daughters remembered. She is about five foot five inches tall. As she grew older she became a trifle round-shouldered, which made her look smaller, but she walked with a firm and confident step. 'Her feet and hands were, and still are models of perfection: above all, she has the most remarkably small and graceful foot I've ever seen; it is rounded and slender but not at all thin; it reminds one of Ariosto's word *ritondetto*.' Her eyes are very black, with a gentle but penetrating gaze, sometimes gay, but more often serious or even severe. She still has all her teeth, which ornament her rare but most charming smile. Her expression is a little fixed, however, as a result of the liquid white make-up she uses, or abuses, to the point of suffering from acute migraines. In short her demeanour is amiable, but sometimes has the remoteness and slight formality of a person of royal blood: Madame Letizia has had no difficulty in getting inside the skin of her role, as we now say. At this time of day she would be playing reversi, a game of which she was passionately fond, with one or two old senators, and we notice that the index finger of her right hand is stiff, probably as the result of the accident she mentioned to Joseph in 1787, which prevented her sewing at the time. She has therefore to manipulate her cards with the other four. The Baronne de Fontanges fills her nostrils with snuff as she listens to anecdotes murmured in her ear by Madame de Fleurieu, 'a stiff, virtuous woman' whose only defect is 'continual chatter, like a tap of tepid water, always turned on and always flowing'. Madame de Bressieux is silent, probably thinking of the time when she was still called Mademoiselle du Colombier, and picked cherries at Valence with young Lieutenant Bonaparte. 'She has a gentle character and engaging ways,' and she watches Madame Mère with as much admiring attention as if she had been the Emperor himself. Magic of the past, nostalgic memories of youth! Madame de Bressieux is not at all like Madame de Saint-Pern, who seems to have accepted the duties of her austere charge on condition she may wail at every opportunity:

'It's for my children ... It's for my children ... for their father.'

The Duc de Cossé-Brissac 'polished, gentle and harmless', but very hump-backed, is deep in an arm-chair, and every time he gets up to leave the room Madame Mère throws an angry glance at him, which the ladies-in-waiting pretend not to notice. 'The poor man is far from suspecting the true cause of his disgrace,' writes Madame d'Abrantès. 'He suffers from constant colic, a disease that is as likely to strike a duke as a serf.' This evening, his wife, the duchess, is playing reversi with Messieurs de Ris, Casabianca and Cholet, whose melancholy, sagging features and wrinkled hands pursue poor Laure d'Abrantès even into her dreams, for she has been on duty as lady-in-waiting in the huge, silent blue drawing-room ever since six o'clock and it will soon be midnight. The good Duchesse de Cossé-Brissac herself is having trouble in hiding her fatigue. This aristocratic lady, a relation of the Duc d'Enghien's wife, has a reputation for wit, but also a slight infirmity which makes it hard to get along with her. All Paris laughed at the story of her presentation to the Emperor. 'She was very anxious to know what questions he would ask and what she should reply. She was told that the Emperor nearly always asked people what department of France they came from, their age and the number of their children. As she was extremely deaf, she mistrusted her own ears, and feared that timidity would only make her failing worse at such a time, so she relied on the Emperor asking her the questions in the order she had been given.' The day of the presentation arrived.

'Is your husband the Brother of the Duc de Brissac who was killed on September 2? Have you inherited his estate?' the Emperor shot at her rapidly.

'Seine-et-Oise,' replied the duchess smiling:
Napoleon's eyebrows went up in surprise, but he continued:
'You have no children?'
'Fifty-two, sire,' with the same smile.
The clock strikes half past eleven. Madame Mère is still deep in reversi.

'I'm so annoyed the Emperor didn't attach you to me instead of my mother-in-law,' Josephine had told Laure d'Abrantès a few days earlier. 'That Household will be very disagreeable for you,

Madame Mère

One of Madame Mère's court dresses

Bust of Madame Mère

I'm sure. Everyone is old, as if part of Louis XV's Court had moved in there. How will you, young and gay as you are, be able to stand that tomb of a place?'

Madame Mère's Household disagreeable? No, but – at midnight everyone at last went off to their rooms, casting an envious glance towards the Tuileries, a centre of life, blazing with lights.

And then, suddenly, the question arose of moving out of Paris, and the whole Household looked far from pleased at the idea. Knowing that his mother liked country air, the Emperor had the idea of installing her in the Dauphin's wing of the Grand Trianon. The Trianon ... deep in the woods ... and miles from Paris ... where there were no distractions except going to mass and playing reversi. Thank heavens, Madame Mère was not attracted by this royal residence. She arrived at Versailles one fine day in May 1805, and found some workmen busy carrying out the Emperor's orders – he had checked the estimate of furnishing and repairs.

'Just look how unsuitably arranged these rooms are,' she exclaimed. 'My bedroom is notoriously inconvenient; there's no dressing-room next door and my women are much too far away. My suite of rooms faces north and is disagreeable and unhealthy.'

All the same, she would consent to install herself in this jewel of pink, green and white marble, which had delighted the hearts of Louis XIV and Louis XV, if they would give her the whole palace, but they objected politely but firmly that the Emperor had kept back those rooms he had not offered her, 'for his own use'. Should she try and make Nabulio relent by speaking of her illness? No, nor had she the time; once more he decided for her. He wrote from Bologna on June 24:

'Madame,

'I have bought the Château of Pont for you. Send your steward to see it and take possession. I shall allow 60,000 francs to furnish it. You will have one of the most beautiful country-places in France; I believe you were there about ten years ago.

It's much finer than Brienne.* I trust you will see in what I have done a fresh proof of my desire to please you.'

He had decided. He was master. But Madame Mère used her 'illness' as a pretext to reply through her secretary, on July 2, 1805:

'Sire,

'Owing to my feelings of extreme weakness after a quite serious illness, I am unable to write to Your Majesty myself, as I would wish, but I do not want to delay expressing my gratitude for the acquisition he has made for me. I write through my secretary to let Your Majesty know that I accept this present, and thank him especially for the kind expressions accompanying it. In that respect, Sire, this evidence of your affection is infinitely touching to me, for you know that your heart is my most precious domain. As soon as I received your letter I sent my steward on his errand, and await the details he brings me to decide what I shall do. I shall certainly go and occupy the property if it is possible.

'Only the thought of your return could keep me in Paris. I hope the sum set aside for repairs and furnishings will be enough. Everything shall be done according to Your Majesty's views. And I shall take care to keep him informed of everything.

'Do not be anxious about my health. The symptoms of my illness were alarming at first; but the care taken of me by Corvisart and my other doctors soon removed them. Exercise and country air will complete my cure. I was not able to go to Trianon, as the arrangements for furnishing it were not complete.

'I have no need to assure you once more, Sire, of an affection which began with your existence and will only end with my own.'

* Remembering the time when, as a poor young cadet, he had been received with slight condescension at the Château of Brienne, he would have liked to own that splendid mansion and besieged Madame Loménie de Brienne to that end.

'Brienne means a lot to me,' he said.

'Sire,' replied the lady, 'Brienne means everything to me.'

He therefore fell back on Pont, which he had often admired at the same period of his life, for its elegance and its situation on the banks of the Seine.

It was indeed a royal present, this imposing Louis XIII chateau, surrounded by two hundred hectares of land and forests; the purchase cost the Emperor 200,000 francs, with 60,000 francs for repairs and furnishing and another 100,000 on his return from Italy plus thirteen Gobelin tapestries. On August 25, Madame Mère arrived at Pont-sur-Seine to take possession of her property, and the villagers' cheerful welcome contrasted with the gloom of the ladies of the Household, who were appalled by being removed so far from Paris, by the isolation and even the lack of shade, as the beautiful trees had been cut down and sold by the owner after the Revolution. 'The life we led at Pont was monotonous and sad, and could be boring for someone of my age,' complained Laure d'Abrantès. Madame Mère, her ladies and her guests, lunched at noon and spent the afternoon doing embroidery or playing the inevitable reversi. Before dinner they paid each other visits, from room to room, and in the cool of the evening they drove round the woods in barouches.

What a contrast with the feverish life of the Tuileries, where the Emperor worked day and night on his plans for the Grand Empire, which was to be the most powerful political system since Charlemagne. The only part Madame Mère played in public affairs was in her capacity as 'Patroness-in-Chief of the Charitable Institutions of the Empire', a post she filled conscientiously, though her piety conflicted with her parsimony ... A witness writes in a deferential tone about the General Council of Sisters of Charity, in 1807: 'The opening of the assembly of the Sisters at the Hôtel de Brienne was presided over by Madame Mère, assisted by the Chief Almoner, with the Abbé Boulogne performing the functions of secretary.' Another states: 'The convent of the Ladies of the Cross was given to the nursing sisters of St. Vincent-de-Paul as the headquarters of their institution at the request of Madame, the Emperor's mother, patroness of all charitable establishments.'

Since nothing escaped the Emperor's notice, and he never missed the opportunity of drawing public attention to the successes of his family, he expressed his satisfaction in a letter published in the *Moniteur de l'Empire*, much as if she had been a general who had just won a campaign:

'Madame,

'I was pleased to read the report on the General Assembly of Sisters of Charity. I have it much at heart to see an increase in the number of houses and individuals concerned in these different institutions, whose object is the relief and care of the sick of my Empire. I have made known to my Minister of Religion my desire for the rules of the different institutions to be revised, and formally defined by my Council within the year . . .

'I can only express my satisfaction at the zeal you have shown, and at these fresh instances of your care. They cannot add to my feelings of veneration and filial love for you.'

Madame Mère's Household laughed up their sleeves seeing all these monks' robes and nuns' coifs, and listened enviously to what the ladies of the Empress' Household or of those of the Princesses Caroline and Pauline had to tell, all of whom had seats in the dress-circle of real events, at balls and receptions instead of in a sort of sewing guild.

The day after Austerlitz they heard that the Emperor was to be proclaimed Emperor of the West . . . At the beginning of 1806 they whispered that Murat, already a marshal and Lord High Admiral, was to be created Grand Duke of Berg, sovereign of a State composed of the duchies of Cleves and Berg . . . What an ascent! Then Joseph, already Grand Elector, was made King of Naples and Sicily, Pauline became Duchesse de Guastalla, and finally Louis, already Constable of the Empire, now sat on the throne of Holland. All this was rather more exciting than Assemblies of the Sisters of Charity . . .

It was while they were marvelling at these events between two games of reversi, that in March Napoleon published his 'Statute defining the law concerning the Family of the Emperor of the French', and dumbfounded Madame Mère and all her Household.

'Her Imperial Highness'

Had the Emperor really been so cruel as to decree that the Imperial Family consisted of princes in their order of seniority, the princesses his sisters and adopted children. And not a word about his mother! Not content with placing all his relations completely in his tyrannical power – the Statute referred to 'arrest, exile and retirement' – he passed in silence over the existence of the one without whom there would have been neither Emperor nor Empire. But there was worse to come . . .

Having decided to marry the niece of Josephine's first husband, Stéphanie de Beauharnais, to the son of the Grand Duke of Baden, whose family turned up their noses at the girl's low rank, he adopted her on the spot – it must be said that she was extremely pretty – gave her the title of Princesse Stéphanie-Napoleon, lodged her in the Tuileries, and made her sit on his right hand, with precedence over the princesses and Madame Mère. What a lesson for the Grand Duke, but what a trial for his own family! Two members of the Beauharnais family (Eugène and this new 'princess') were now married into royal families, and Hortense was mother of the child who was said to be the Emperor's heir – it was really too much, and the Bonaparte clan were reunited as if by magic and choking with rage. Caroline pretended to faint when she saw the 'adopted daughter' enter a drawing-room in front of her. Madame Mère's ladies, bored to extinction at Pont, gloated over this development. And then . . . and then, early in 1806, their faces brightened, for it was whispered between two stitches of embroidery that the Emperor had agreed to increase his mother's allowance, from 300,000 to 480,000 francs. Not that this could wipe out the affront unwittingly inflicted by the 'adopted daughter'. So Madame Mère tightened her purse-strings a little, and allowed it to be put about – hoping it might reach the Emperor's ears – that she had the reputation of being 'miserly'. By dint of brooding over her wrongs, and wearing an aggrieved, even angry, expression, she succeeded in attracting the attention of Nabulio, who finally asked her one day what would please her.

After consultation, her private secretary devised a letter which, though it aimed at resembling an official document, was in fact as tortuous as a draft agreement – the very essence of the sort of screed that infuriated Napoleon.

'Paris, May 9, 1806

'Sire,

'When Your Majesty asked me to let him know what would please me, I thought at first that I should leave it to his wisdom and affection for me. What can I ask of one who knows everything, foresees everything and can command everything? However, riper reflection has convinced me that I should not leave him in further doubt about my views and my true feelings. I will therefore explain myself with the frankness that is inseparable from the intimate communications of the heart, and in which personal calculations necessarily have no part.

'At my age and in my position, I cannot have any ambitious pretensions. All my happiness lies in that of my family. Everything Your Majesty does to make the family glorious affects me personally. I ought not, nor do I wish to aspire to a similar destiny; reason and taste would prevent me, even if I did not find satisfaction in my position. My title of the Emperor's mother is glory enough; my place at your side is as distinguished in my eyes as it is dear to my heart.

'In that respect, I desire no change from the present state of things. I have only one wish: to witness your glory, and your happiness for many years to come. But I must maintain as dignified a life in the Empire as is suitable to my rank.

'It is less for myself than for you that I wish this, because Your Majesty's mother should be honoured by all nations, as much as you yourself honour and love her, and you know how much external splendour adds to that of titles or even of personal qualities in the eyes of public opinion.

'You therefore should consider, Sire, whether my allowance is sufficient in relation to the obligations imposed by my position, and whether the form it takes is a fitting one. An income of

480,000 francs is certainly enough for my personal needs; in relation to my political position it is not. A display of suitable dignity requires greater means.

'I should fail to maintain that suitable display if my suite were not at least on a level with that of other members of the imperial family, and if I were to reduce my manner of providing for my Household.

'I therefore need, firstly, the necessary measures to provide me with supplies of china, linen and furniture that I have been unable to procure from my present revenue. You know, Sire, that I received nothing to cover the first expenses of my establishment. I also need a fixed revenue, proportionate to the constant maintenance of honourable appearances. You have points of comparison by which to judge what I need. Your noble feelings will also indicate to you what degree of splendour should surround the mother of the most powerful monarch in the world.

'Notice also, Sire, that to keep up a display worthy of us both requires an increase in my Household of honour. I can even say that this is as much a matter of my own feelings as it is of suitability, that the members of my Household share the advantages of an elevation of the dignity of their functions, and that in serving me they find a special title to Your Majesty's goodwill. Furthermore, this increase in their numbers would be a return to the rules that have always established differences in the organisation of Households, according to rank and proximity to the princes of royal blood.

'As to the manner of settling my allowance, I would suggest you reflect upon the following points:

'A simple pension, not determined by a deed nor clothed in legal terms, offers me valuable evidence of your love, but does not give me a definite title emanating from the sovereign power. In your feelings for me I have the safest guarantee of my actual fate, but I declare, Sire, that at no time and in no circumstances do I wish to be dependent on your will, and your tender foresight cannot fail to desire and ordain it accordingly. To fix my allowance thus seems to me to be consonant with Your Majesty's feelings as much as with my personal dignity.

'I am not afraid to go further and to admit, Sire, that it would be sweet to me to be glorified in a solemn act which would show the French nation the feelings you profess for me, and which have up to this moment constituted the charm of my private life.

'Ancient laws have assigned the annual dower of a queen mother to be supplied from public contributions. Whatever differences may spring from my particular position, the principle on which these laws are based is not absolutely irrelevant to me. A senatus consultum assigns to your brothers an income appanaged upon the Public Treasury. The great dignitaries of the Empire have received the same distinction. Do you not think that it would become Your Majesty to arrange for the same measure to function in my case? Believe me, Sire, that all Frenchmen, all fathers of families, would be moved by such an act of filial piety. Your laws tend towards re-establishing the domestic virtues; you would certainly influence them by such a noble example.

'I am sure that in these circumstances the highest body in the State would grant you a fresh proof of its devotion, and that after so often paying the tribute of their admiration to your public virtues, they would show tenderness in offering a similar veneration to your private virtues.

'Further, Sire, if other elements than sentiment can be combined with the idea I submit to you, I beg you to note that the elevation of your brother to the throne of Naples may bring his allowance in France to an end, and make the charge on my behalf less burdensome for the Public Treasury; also that as my life is nearing its end an annual allowance cannot offer a heavy call on the State's resources, and finally that my unique position in your family means that nothing personal to me can be taken as an example.

'This, Sire, is everything I can wish for. I am happy in my present position and I do not conceal what enchantment has entered my life from possessing such a son as you. But when I

'Her Imperial Highness'

suggest that you should give my life even more brilliance, it is not vain pleasures I am seeking: you can surely see that these ideas spring from maternal feelings which cannot separate my glory from your own.'

The secretary had taken a great deal of trouble to muffle up in rhetoric the gist of his argument – namely, that the Emperor was mortal, that he might be killed in war, and that it was therefore advisable that his mother's allowance should be inscribed in the Great Book of State, and so guaranteed ... Nabulio must have fumed as he read this terribly pompous, grandiloquent and erudite letter, having so little resemblance to the woman who had signed it – except perhaps in the details concerning china and linen, and also its insistence on the title of Empress-Mother, which would give her precedence over all the Beauharnais in Europe ...

This demand received no written reply! Perhaps Nabulio had an explanation with his mother during one of those Sunday dinners at the Tuileries, when the whole family gathered. It is only known that he agreed to a present of 600,000 francs in August. No question of statutes, rights and prerogatives, making Madame Letizia the head of the dynasty. She owed her place to the position of her son – who could only pass on his title to his own issue – and she would never enjoy any situation except such as he accorded her out of pure courtesy and love.

* * *

Her great diplomatic negotiation having failed, Madame Mère went off to sulk at Pont, whence she resumed her correspondence with Lucien, joining her efforts to those of his children and his brother to bring about a reconciliation between the Emperor and the voluntary exile. An inventory of Lucien's papers shows that during the years of 1806 and 1807 alone there were about a hundred letters from his family on Napoleon's favourite theme of 'everything for Lucien divorced; nothing for Lucien married'.

The truth, as Madame Mère knew, was that Nabulio hoped to

employ the rebel – the ablest of his brothers and most naturally gifted for politics – but *caro Luciano* was committing a thousand rash acts under the protection of the Papal States, as if his sole object were to defy him and exhibit his opposition to the Empire.

'We often talk of you,' his mother wrote in September 1806, 'and your position is henceforth the only thing that torments my heart, which is without other cause for pain. That is what forces me to repeat over and over that you ought to show the greatest possible discretion and reserve both in any conversations you may have and in letters, written to anyone at all.'

Cardinal Fesch was, perhaps naturally, too much inclined to preach at Lucien, and his theatrical emphasis gained him a volley of sharp retorts, administered with all the energy of a revolutionary orator: 'You seem to have forgotten honour as well as religion ... At least have the good sense not to liken me to Jerome, and spare me the useless shame of your cowardly advice. In a word – stop writing to me until religion and honour, which you are trampling underfoot, have dispelled your blindness ... At least hide your ignoble feelings beneath your purple, and make your way along the wide road of ambition in silence.' Madame Mère thought that things had changed indeed; letters in this style would never have been written to the uncle archdeacon – and what was an archdeacon compared to a Cardinal and primate of Gaul! It was she who answered this insolent note on November 2, 1806: 'I have received the reply I was waiting for so anxiously, but how different it is from what I had hoped for. God wills it so, and I am destined to pass my life in sadness and desolation; I will never again speak to you about this subject, and in future I will merely deplore your disgrace and mine in my thoughts. Fesch told me how you wrote to him. I cannot help saying I think you have treated him very badly.'

So the bridges were broken, and a whole year was to pass before Nabulio and Luciano finally met, only to quarrel and break off relations definitely. Being on bad terms with this much loved son was the chief source of Signora Letizia's unhappiness during 1807, the year which saw the meeting on a raft between the Tsar of all the Russias, Alexander I, and the Emperor of the French, King of Italy, Mediator of the Swiss Confederation, Protector of the Confederation of the Rhine, Napoleon I – Nabulio. The year which was to bring the names of hitherto unknown villages – Eylau, Friedland and Tilsit – into the pages of history and see them embroidered on banners.

The Emperor was far away and Madame Mère was deprived of these visits that plunged the Hôtel de Brienne into agitation and terrified the ladies-in-waiting and companions: the sound of horses hooves on the paved courtyard, several shouts of 'Long live the Emperor' from passers-by, the quick step of a man in boots coming up the stone staircase four steps at a time. She would just have time to send away her visitors or her readers before Nabulio came in like a whirlwind and kissed her on the forehead.

'Good morning, Mother.'

'Good morning, my son.'

What did they talk about, as she sat erect in her large arm-chair upholstered in purple velvet and gold braid, and he walked up and down with his hands behind his back, or stood by the window looking on to the marvellous garden with its smoothly raked alleys? Of the Casa Bonaparte, Milelli, the Capitello tower, Toulon, Marseilles, and the road they had travelled since then ... She looked at him with eyes full of love and admiration. He was in such a good humour that day.

'What enchantment having a son such as you has brought to my life!'

'It's to you, to your good principles that I owe my good fortune and any good I may have done.'

But another day his expression would be stern.

'How are you liking it at Court, Signora Letizia? You're bored, aren't you? Well, that's because you don't know how to enjoy life. You don't throw open your drawing-rooms. Look at your daughters: they seem to have been born into their present positions. I've given you a town mansion and a fine country estate, plus an allowance of a million, and you live like a bourgeoise from St. Denis. You mustn't hoard what I give you; spend it.'

'In that case you'll have to give me two millions instead of one, because I can't help saving; it's my nature.'

They laughed.

'Goodbye, Mother.'

'Goodbye, my son.'*

Now that he was so far away, Paris, capital of Europe, was no longer the same town. Ministers became idle, enemies raised their heads, important persons plotted and planned, and the royalist drawing-rooms produced witticisms. As for Madame Mère, she had difficulty in chasing away the thoughts that obsessed her and made her turn pale whenever a dusty courier alighted before the steps of her house.

'A single shot could kill him. God is not obliged to perform miracles to save him.'

That winter of 1806–7, the winter of Napoleon's victorious entry into Berlin and Warsaw, was spent by Madame Mère at the Hôtel de Brienne; she was planning to improve it. 'I've decided to have my yellow salon on the ground floor gilded,' she wrote to the Cardinal, 'and the work is already in progress, but I need something to go over four of the doors. Simon tells me that you have some paintings by Benedetto di Castiglione and that they would go well there. If you will let me have three I will pay you back with other, better pictures, that you have shown signs of wanting.'

January 1807 saw a strange set-to-partners in the family. Napoleon met the beautiful and touching Countess Walewska and made her his mistress, writing to Josephine who was awaiting his return at Mainz: 'Paris is asking for you; go there, I wish it.' The

---

* 'Madame was altogether too frugal,' Napoleon was to say at St. Helena. 'It was ridiculous. Basically it was only excess of precaution on her part; she was afraid of finding herself with nothing some day: she had known poverty and could never forget those terrible days. Besides, it is fair to say that she gave a great deal to her children in secret; she was a good mother.' Madame of d'Abrantès: *Mémoires*.

Empress set off and reached the Tuileries on January 31, armed with the Emperor's instructions: 'Be worthy of me ... Keep up a suitable state in Paris.' A few days later she received a note announcing the Battle of Eylau. 'My dear, there was a great battle; the victory fell to me, but my losses have been grave ... I am writing you these two lines myself, although I am very tired, to tell you that I am well and I love you.'

A great battle? There were rumours going round Paris that Eylau had been above all a scene of horrible butchery, that the Emperor had been close to disaster, that his star had begun to wane, and the Empress – red-eyed – found it very difficult to keep up a suitable state in such circumstances. 'You let yourself be distressed by the remarks of the very people who ought to comfort you. I advise you to show a little spirit, and to know how to put everyone in his place,' ordered Napoleon. Fine words! She was hardly installed in the Tuileries when her mother-in-law announced that she was going to retire to Pont for the summer months – obviously a means of avoiding making an appearance at Court. Poor Madame Mère, it needed considerable independence to make up her mind when to move. An order arrived from Finkenstein, where Nabulio was preparing his campaign against Russia and making love to Maria Walewska. 'Madame, I completely approve of your going to the country, but, while you are in Paris it is proper that you dine every Sunday with the Empress, at her family dinner. My family is a political one. When I am away the Empress is always the head of it. Besides, it is an honour I bestow on the members of my family. That will not prevent me from coming to dine with you, whenever I happen to be in Paris and my occupations allow.'

Thus severely reprimanded, Madame Mère remained in Paris, thanking God that Josephine had gone off to Malmaison, St. Cloud and then Brussels, so that she could escape the burdensome duty of Sundays at the Tuileries. In May 1807, the death of the eldest son of Louis and Hortense, the Emperor's heir-presumptive – the first mourning suffered by the Empire – dismayed her, but chiefly on account of the poor 'King' of Holland, who was dragging his sufferings and the bad temper of a neurasthenic valetudinarian between palaces and spas.

Napoleon returned to St. Cloud in a halo of glory from Friedland and Tilsit on July 27, 1807, and on August 15 he ordered a Te Deum to be celebrated on the occasion of his birthday and to give thanks for peace – a ceremony attended by Madame Mère. 'The Empress, very gracious, well-dressed and in stately style, was in the transept,' noted the Countess Potocka, 'but the only person I had eyes for was the Emperor's mother. There she was, the happiest of women, from whom no reverses, no hostile power, can take away the glory of having given birth to the most extraordinary man the passing centuries have produced. How proud she must be! A great crowd of people bowing before her son, and the vaults ringing with their acclamations. It is the finest role in the world for a woman. She is beautiful, still looks young: one would never guess she was his mother.'

A few days later, Prince Jerome was the sole subject of conversation – Jerome whose divorce 'on grounds of minority' had been pronounced, Jerome who had been promoted to rear-admiral and lieutenant-general, Jerome who hadn't given the faintest subsequent cause for worry, and whose letters to the Emperor declared either: 'I love nothing in the world as I do Your Majesty,' or 'It will be my glory and happiness to deserve Your Majesty's approval by my conduct.' He had just been 'nominated' King of Westphalia, he was engaged to Catherine, daughter of the King of Würtemberg, and the future husband and wife met at the Château of Raincy, home of the Junots, on the evening of August 21. The princess, who was rather 'stout' – the adjective is a euphemism – short and with very little neck, devoured with her eyes the tall, slim, handsome Jerome, with his profile like a Roman coin, brilliant smile and sparkling eyes, as he recited the sentence Napoleon had probably prepared for him:

'My brother is waiting for us, I do not want to delay his pleasure in getting to know the new sister I am giving him.'

The civil wedding was celebrated next day in the Gallery of Diana at the Tuileries, in the presence of about eight hundred members of the Court, and the painter Regnault made sketches for his historic painting: the Emperor and Empress on a dais, Madame Mère on her son's left, sitting in an arm-chair – a special distinction, the prince and princesses of the Family having ordinary chairs. Before signing the contract, Jerome, looking exceptionally elegant in a suit of white satin embroidered in the French style, came forward and bowed to the Emperor and his mother, to beg their consent, which was given with signs of the head. Princess Catherine had been brought up in an austere German court; she was dazzled by the sight of jewellery to the value of 600,000 francs, and the lingerie and dresses among her wedding-presents.*

After these Parisian festivities, the whole Court moved to Fontainebleau. 'The Court was more brilliant than that of Louis XIV had ever been,' said Madame d'Abrantès. During the hunting parties, picnics, huge dinners and theatrical performances, the guests' eyes were fixed on Josephine, for the rumours of divorce current for some time were beginning to take shape.

'*They* won't be happy until *they* have sent me away from the French throne ... *They*'re all against me,' wailed the Empress.

'*They*' were the Bonapartes, who had just discovered that time had been on their side and against 'the old woman', as they called her: ever since he had had a son by one of Queen Caroline's readers in 1806, thus proving his capacity for procreation, Napoleon had been dreaming of divorce, and often glanced through the lists of the 'available' European princesses, trying to make a choice.

* 'The Emperor himself gave me chemises,' the princess confessed, getting rid of the old-fashioned lingerie she had brought from Stuttgart. She didn't forget, for she was well-bred – a descendant of Frederick the Great – and even after the battle of Waterloo, she obstinately defended her brother-in-law when he fell into English hands. Her attitude came to the ears of the exile on St. Helena, who commented simply: 'The princess has written her own name on the pages of History.'

One morning there was general amazement at the news that the Emperor had left before dawn, at four o'clock, on a journey whose object and destination were unknown. While every sort of supposition was being canvassed, he was rumbling in his travelling-coach along the road leading to Italy – to Milan, where he was to meet Lucien. Madame Mère was exultant for more than one reason. This meeting was the result of her labours, but also she had just been granted the appanaged allowance of a million francs, which she had hankered after for so long, Nabulio having transferred to her the sum allowed to Jerome, who as King of Westphalia was provided for by the civil list paid for by his subjects. She had been scheming to bring about this meeting for several months, often signing letters to Lucien dictated by Joseph, or saying that Nabulio was well-disposed towards him, which was a complete fable. 'Joseph has written to me from Bologna that he found the Emperor better disposed towards you, and that you had gone to meet him. This news pleased and contented me very much,' she wrote to *caro Luciano* on December 28. 'Ever since that time I have been, and still am, in the greatest anxiety to hear the result of your conversation, but your silence on such an important matter, on which as you know my happiness depends, is beginning to destroy all the high hopes I had conceived, since I'm sure you wouldn't have delayed for a single instant letting me know if a complete reconciliation had been the result.'

She was right. The meeting took place at Mantua on the night of December 12 to 13. We have three versions of those six crowded hours, between which a historian moves as in a maze, making the most of one or two landmarks here and there.

'Don't unharness the horses,' Lucien ordered his companions on the journey. 'I may leave again this evening.'

'Well, what have you got to say to me?' Napoleon asked him.

'Sire, I am waiting to hear what Your Majesty wishes to tell me.'

Poor Madame Mère, who had done her best to convince

Nabulio that Luciano was ready to make the first move, and that Nabulio was similarly disposed. Right from the beginning both brothers adhered to their former positions.

'Choose any kingdom you please,' Napoleon said tersely, unrolling a map of Europe... 'Louis is as obstinate as a mule and Jerome as incapable as a child... So you are the one I rest all my hopes on.'

'Before going into this explanation further,' retorted Lucien, 'I must tell you that I have not changed at all.'

'You must understand my system... follow my footprints.'

'I don't sell myself.'

'Always the same... always the same... Why have you come to see me then?'

'I'm not your subject... I will never give in.'

'Think... night brings counsel. Till tomorrow then.'

Lucien nodded, seemed about to speak, then partly opening the door rushed out of the room, got back into his carriage and left that very moment.

Madame Mère at once sent her approval of his proud reaction. 'I'm pleased to see that you decided to refuse the honours you were offered, and to retire into the country: your position demands it and if you hadn't informed me of your intention I would have been the first to advise it.' As usual she secretly sided with the loser of the battle, if only because he was the weakest, but she sighed as she signed this letter, because never, never at all, had the relations between the members of her family been so bad. Hortense had just left Louis, getting all the blame, principally because she was a Beauharnais and because she was on the point of embarking on a *liaison raisonnée* with young General de Flahaut, but people pretended to forget how much patience she had needed to put up with the presence of a neurotic husband for six years – a husband who got into bed on their wedding night wearing a night-shirt of a man with an itch, so as to 'draw out his morbid humours'. Jerome committed a thousand indiscretions, behaving like a king in an operetta and squandering a fifth of the revenues of his kingdom on his daily expenses. And it may have been at this time that the conversation took place which Madame Mère describes in her *Souvenirs*:

'The Emperor was complaining of all his brothers, He said: "I'll have this one locked up... that one arrested." I said: "My son, you are both right and wrong: right if you compare them to yourself, because you cannot be compared to anyone in the world, you're a marvel, a phenomenon, unique. But you are wrong if you compare them to other kings, because they are better than them all; because other kings are so stupid that they seem to wear veils over their eyes, and their fall was necessary so that my children could replace them."

'The Emperor heard me out and said:

'"Signora Letizia" – he was laughing – "so even you flatter me?"

'"I flatter you? You do your mother an injustice. A mother doesn't flatter her son. You know, Sire, that in public I treat you with all possible respect, because I'm your subject; but in private I am your mother and you are my son, and so when you say: 'I wish it,' I reply, 'I don't wish it.'"'

This wasn't the whole story, however. When she got Canova to make a statue of her – exhibited in the Salon of 1808 – she had the idea of putting this masterpiece in the Tuileries, in a position where the Emperor and the whole Court would have it always in view – namely in the Throne room, exactly opposite the throne. This time it was Nabulio's turn to say, 'I don't wish it.'

The marble was placed in the Gallery of Diana. It didn't suit the Emperor to stress the fact that his dynasty sprang from any other person but himself.

When the Emperor left for Erfurt, where the Tsar was awaiting him, Madame Mère plunged into her favourite occupation of financial calculation, happy in the security given by a dowry of a million, and a present of 600,000 francs. She had obtained this munificent settlement by parading her difficulties in maintaining her Household in fitting state, and she now made the best of things by ordering a silver-gilt dinner-service, which remained in

'Her Imperial Highness'

its case because she could never make up her mind to give receptions! Supported by her millions, marvelling at her good fortune, she naïvely confided in various people such comments as the following, stuffed with delicious Corsican turns of speech:

'The Emperor tells me I am a (*jou souis oune*) villain, but I (*ma jou*) let him talk. He says that I never give anyone food (*mangiare*); but if he wants me to keep an inn, let him give me a Household such as the mother of an Emperor and three kings should have – with pages, stewards and chamberlains. Then he'll see whether I don't do the honours with proper dignity.'

Or again:

'I am obliged to plan (*coumouler*) for the future. My son has a fine position, but (*ma*) that may not last (*dourer*) for ever. Who knows whether all these kings won't come to me begging for bread some day.'

Her plans for saving by steering a middle course, so to speak, out of fear of some remote contingency, enabled her to amass a fortune of about 14 million francs, on which everyone tried to draw, when bad times came later. Avarice? It was more like a sense of order, whose first manifestation was economy. After all, Goethe found time to note down in his account book the price of Göttingen sausages, to weigh every morsel of bread, and sleep with the key of the wood-shed under his pillow. And Madame Mère was wonderfully good at passing off her frugality as simplicity, by hiring books from a lending library and making savage cuts in her expenses, as she did when she was running the Casa Bonaparte. As for scattering presents everywhere, like those brainless kings...

'Madame de Fontanges, who was only moderately well off, possessed no cashmere shawl, so someone remarked to Madame Mère. A few days later, when she arrived to take up her duties, Madame showed her one, woven of exquisite material.

'"What do you think of it?"

'"Very beautiful, Madame, and the colour is charming."

'"I'm delighted you like it, because it's yours."

'Madame de Fontagnes thought is was a present. But the illusion was short-lived. Next day she was brought the bill by the merchant from whom the shawl had been purchased for her.'*

* * *

While the Emperor was confiscating provinces belonging to the Holy See – and earning excommunication thereby – and while he was making war against Spain, so as to install Joseph on the throne of Madrid, or galloping to Erfurt to renew his alliance with the Tsar; while he took a second journey to Spain to beat the English, and attempt to consolidate the royal house he had imposed on the Spaniards much against their will; while he was reflecting in his travelling-coach, on horse-back or in his tent as to what preparations he could make to prevent being surprised by Austria's declaration of war in April 1809, Madame Mère renewed her active correspondence with *caro Luciano*, who, having agreed to give the Pope 100,000 piastres for the relief of the hard-pressed Vatican Treasury, received in exchange the estate of Canino, birth-place of Paul III Farnese. The chief subject of these letters was young Charlotte Bonaparte, Lucien's daughter by his first wife, born in 1796 and now a little over twelve; there was a question of bringing her to Paris and installing her in the Hôtel de Brienne.

This devious plot had been hatched during the interview at Mantua: to Napoleon the little girl was merely a pawn, a hand to be bestowed on some prince, eager (or compelled) to enter the 'system', perhaps the Prince of the Asturias, son of the King of Spain; on the other hand Lucien had added two years to his daughter's age so as to make her more 'interesting', more politically useful, and it was a question of making the most of her by securing her a position at Court in the Tuileries. Alas! when he got home Lucien realised that among Nabulio's associates little Charlotte would hear more than one disagreeable comment on her step-mother, 'the hussy' or 'the concubine', and about her

* *Anecdotes sur la Cour de la Famille de Napoléon Bonaparte* (1818).

brothers by the second marriage, 'the bastards', and changed his mind in consequence, but Madame Mère returned to the attack on December 6, 1808. 'The Emperor complains that you haven't carried out what you *promised* at your last meeting, and sent your daughter to Paris; he adds that it depends on you whether you become a reigning monarch like your brothers; that he isn't insisting on your leaving your wife and children. You can live with them and he will impose no conditions regarding a new marriage; only he cannot recognise the one you have contracted. From his frank and easy way of talking, as well as from his filial and brotherly tone, I don't think I'm mistaken in saying that he only wants that one satisfaction to give you his friendship again; time will settle everything else. Now, after much reflection, I think you should comply with his wishes, for your own sake and for that of your children and your family. I think your wife ought to agree to this... Remember that the sorrow you cause me is shortening my life as much as the passing years, and when I am dead and gone there will be no means of reconciliation... Always putting things off only makes them more difficult. Make up your mind, it's a favourable moment... Don't let pride hold you back. The Emperor is a father to us all and he has the right to expect satisfaction from his brothers.'

This letter had no effect on *caro Luciano*, whose dream it was to put the ocean between himself and his terrible brother and whose wallet contained passports for the United States, issued by the English consul at Cagliari in the form of a guarantee that the Royal Navy would not oppose his voyage. Then came the great events of the summer of 1809 and everything else faded into the background.

On April 12 Napoleon received by telegraph the news of Austria's declaration of war.

'I'll start in two hours,' he said simply.

The master of lightning warfare left Paris next day at four o'clock in the morning. On the 22nd he beat the Austrians at Eckmühl, and on May 13 at two o'clock in the morning Vienna capitulated. Napoleon moved into the capital, and the proof of his power is that he carried on the administration of his Empire from there for some time. On the 17th he signed 'from his Imperial camp at Vienna', the decree joining the Papal States to the French Empire. History was advancing by giant strides. On July 6, while cannon were thundering in the plains of Wagram, the Pope was arrested and taken to Savona. What confusion in the Courts of Europe!

Madame Mère and Pauline went calmly off to take the waters at Aix-la-Chapelle. They were in high spirits, for the news of the victory of Wagram had reached them the day before their departure, and astonishingly enough Madame forgot to complain of the cost of living away from home, and smiled when her daughter burst out laughing.*

One of the Empire's important officials, Comte Beugnot, administrator of the Grand Duchy of Berg, came to pay his respects. 'Madame asked me to tell her in detail what expenses I had incurred in arriving and staying at the spa,' he wrote in his *Mémoires*. 'I hadn't the faintest idea. For me, as for most people, it was a matter for my valet to see to. I answered at random, and kept reducing the amount, so as to give Madame Mère a good impression of my practical sense; unfortunately she took my boasting for current prices. That very day she started a campaign against her servants and her suppliers; she maintained both were robbing her shamefully, giving me as an example of someone who wasn't being treated in this deplorable fashion; she named the articles and the prices I had paid for them; it was impossible to budge her. However, General Beurnonville, who had witnessed one of the many scenes of which I had been the unwitting cause,

---

* Ferdinand de Lariboisière, page to the Emperor, galloped for three days and nights without sleep to bring the news, and appeared before the Empress and Pauline holding his hat 'tightly pressed against his back', because he had worn through the seat of his breeches. Josephine rewarded him with a diamond, Pauline with a smile.

'That doesn't surprise me in the least,' said Napoleon teasingly when he heard these details, 'Pauline is a silly girl.'

explained to Madame that I was not at all well versed in domestic matters, and that this was a subject in which I had very little authority. Madame stuck to her guns, but asked me to call again. I postponed this second visit as long as I could, but an invitation to dinner put me in a tight corner; I had to go, and take up our discussion where it left off. I hadn't prepared my case properly. Whether to further her own plans or merely out of malice, Madame again put me through the items of expenditure at Aix-la-Chapelle, praised my cleverness to the skies, and begged me to procure the articles we had spoken of and pay for them on her behalf, at the same prices that I myself had paid.'

The Emperor would have enjoyed hearing his mother give a lesson on economy to an important personage who thought financial problems beneath his notice, because it was from her that he had inherited his mania for keeping everything under his personal control, even the details of his clothes, as well as his hatred of profiteers, which often caused him to protest:

'Why should it be dearer for me than anyone else? I don't understand that. Must I be robbed?'

Apart from this, Beugnot was much impressed by the illustrious visitor to the spa. 'Madame Mère was between fifty and fifty-five, and as beautiful as a woman of that age can be . . . She had wit and sound common sense, and didn't let herself be dazzled by her position.'

Madame Mère and Pauline returned to Paris that autumn to present themselves at Fontainebleau, where the Emperor arrived on October 26. A few days before, at Vienna, a young man called Stabs had tried to assassinate him, and this event acted as a reminder that his vast empire was at the mercy of such a criminal, that he must therefore have an heir and that Josephine must be sacrificed.

'While there is no direct heir,' said the Arch-Chancellor the cold-hearted Cambacérès emphatically, 'the country can have no confidence in its future.'

* * *

On December 15, 1809, at nine o'clock in the evening, the most important personages of the State foregathered in the Throne Room at the Tuileries: the Princes of the Empire, members of the Privy Council, all in order of precedence; Madame Mère, more unbending than usual with her impassive face thickly covered in white powder, Louis, Jerome, Murat, Eugène and their wives; then the women, Hortense, Catherine, Pauline and Caroline, all wearing decorations. They were received by the Emperor and Empress, seated in arm-chairs behind a table loaded with papers and inkpots. Everyone sat down in silence. Then there arrived the Arch-Chancellor of the Empire, Cambacérès, and the Secretary of State of the Imperial House, Regnault de St. Jean d'Angély, and Napoleon stood up – he was wearing the uniform of a colonel of the Guard, and read aloud the declaration prepared by Maret, his Minister-Secretary of State, which he had re-phrased so as to give it a more human, even a tenderer tone. It explained the political necessity of divorce, and lingered for some time on the bonds of affection attaching him to the Empress.

'God knows what such a decision has cost my heart. But there is no sacrifice beyond my courage when it has been shown that it is for the good of France ... I have nothing but praise for the support and devotion of my beloved wife ... I wish her to keep the rank and title of crowned Empress, but above all that she should never doubt my sentiments, and that she always looks upon me as her best and dearest friend.'

Josephine, dressed in white without jewels, and with her hair held back by a ribbon, stood up in turn, the very image of sacrifice. She too had seen the official document, and had inserted some graceful phrases emphasising her pain.

'With the permission of my august and beloved husband, I must declare that, since I have no further hope of having children to satisfy political needs and the interests of France, I am pleased to give him the greatest proof of attachment and devotion that has ever been given on this earth ...'

Her voice was stifled by sobs, her strength deserted her, and

'Her Imperial Highness'

she collapsed sobbing into her chair. Regnault de St. Jean d'Angély finished reading for her:

'Everything I have comes from his goodness: it was his hand that crowned me, and on the height of that throne I have received nothing but evidence of affection and love from the French people... Both of us are proud of the sacrifice we are making for the good of our country.'

When the Emperor pressed the hand of the woman from whom he was parting, Madame Mère wiped her eyes. Nevertheless... Only three days earlier she had sent Lucien a victorious bulletin: 'The Emperor is going to divorce the Empress. The decision has been made and will very soon be announced. It is only a question of form. Louis is also separating from his wife, but without a divorce. He is staying with me. His health is better than usual. I think I can state with assurance that the Emperor's feelings for his family are already quite different from before. Don't be obstinate, my dear son, and do begin by doing what is asked of you. I hope that before long we shall all be content. What a consolation it would be for me if I could see you here, and embrace you with the rest of the family.'

Ever since she had been certain that Josephine was going to be set aside, she had been having long confabulations with Fesch and Pauline, whose purpose was nothing more nor less than to arrange a marriage between Nabulio and Lucien's daughter Charlotte, and she seemed firmly resolved to carry this plan through, for Elisa, who had joined the conspiracy, was already suggesting to the exile at Canino: 'Up till now, I had no suspicion as to who might be the Emperor's new wife; if my desires were fulfilled this choice would put an end to a disagreement which has caused me heartfelt pain.' Charlotte was only fifteen, but Madame Mère was already a mother at that age, and besides the important thing was that the new empress would be a Bonaparte and not an 'outsider'. It was really unthinkable that Lucien shouldn't receive a throne in exchange for his daughter! Campi, the Corsican who had remained faithfully devoted to both

Madame Mère and Lucien, was to go to and fro between Paris and Canino to further this strange project.

Lucien thought his position must have improved now that there was a demand for his daughter, and suddenly got on to his high horse: the bonds he had formed with Madame Jouberthon were 'indissoluble' until death. While he was arguing and storming, news came that Austria had agreed to bestow the hand of the Archduchess Marie-Louise, eldest daughter of the Emperor Francis I, upon Napoleon, and the burning question of the journey to Paris and marriage of Charlotte – always called Lolotte in the family – faded into the background. There remained the question of a reconciliation between the two brothers, so dear to Madame Mère's heart, and this appeared in a very unpromising light when Campi was summoned to the Tuileries one day in February 1810, and the storm broke.

'Let Lucien consider well,' thundered Napoleon: 'does he intend to leave his wife or not? If he comes here with all his children I will forget his misdeeds and restore him to his proper rank. Does he prefer his wife to his children's happiness, peace in the family, and all the great plans I have conceived? Then he is no longer my brother, I don't wish to hear him mentioned; he can go to America... If I am compelled to sacrifice him I shall do so without the slightest difficulty. They tell me that since his retirement he has taken to study; he must therefore be familiar with the history of those who have founded empires, as I have done.'

As for Lolotte, let her come. Campi was amazed... who would look after her?

'As things are between the Emperor and me,' wailed Madame Mère, 'what shall I do with her if she comes?'

'Mama said that to you?' said Napoleon in surprise. 'Mama will do her duty. She will look after her grand-daughter. Ah! it's her avarice again'...

On March 8 the little girl arrived at the Hôtel de Brienne in Paris. 'As soon as she has been fitted out,' Madame Mère told Lucien, 'I will take her to see the Emperor, and I'm convinced she will be well received. I'll write and tell you the next day. God grant that I can at the same time announce the one thing lacking to make me happy – a reconciliation between you.'

With what ingenuous zeal she and the Cardinal were scheming to force Nabulio's hand: they were now trying to make Lolotte's arrival seem like a first step on Lucien's part towards repudiating his wife, just at the very moment when Campi returned from Canino with a letter rejecting any such idea.

'Very well,' grumbled Napoleon, 'that's the end of the matter ... Why on earth did Mama and Fesch come and tell me only yesterday that Lucien would arrange a divorce?'

'I don't understand any of it,' complained Campi. 'When I arrived, Madame Mère and the Cardinal told me that Your Majesty was no longer insisting on divorce ... This is how Monsieur Lucien has been deceived by his own relations for the last year.'

'Then my relations have deceived both Lucien and me,' concluded Napoleon.*

When he left the audience-chamber, Campi hurried to the Hôtel de Brienne to complain of being the victim of double-dealing, but he was taken aback to find Madame Mère had gone over to the other side, along with Fesch and Pauline. She swore she had never spoken of divorce but only separation – civil divorce in which the church would have had no part ... that Nabulio had agreed ... that Lucien had no reason to refuse ... that the children would be recognised.

'The Emperor is acting in good faith. He will never force Lucien to marry again ... If Lucien doesn't snatch at this chance I shall begin thinking that he's become an enemy of the family, or else gone completely off his head.'†

Perhaps, with her peasant good sense tinged with Italian craftiness, she had come to the conclusion that Lucien's position was untenable, when confronted with Nabulio whom the exercise

* F. Masson: *Napoléon et sa famille*.
† Ibid.

of power was every day making more authoritarian and inaccessible to ordinary feelings. This appears to be the explanation of the letter she sent a few days later to Madame Lucien, a woman she had been fond of and protected, and whose child she had held at the baptismal font: 'You are aware of all the unhappiness that your marriage has brought upon our family. The Emperor is set upon your divorce; only you can persuade Lucien to arrange it, and should he refuse, it is for you to ask him for one. It's the only means of avoiding the disgrace that threatens him and everyone belonging to you . . . Lastly, if you have any consideration for a mother who has always been ready to make sacrifices for her children, you will do this for me also, and I assure you I will remember it all my life.' She entrusted this letter to Campi who was just leaving for Canino, adding a remark which sums her up completely:

'A father and mother who cannot sacrifice themselves for their children do not deserve the name.'

Her last move, a letter to *caro Luciano* betrays her distress and indignation, her wounded pride and her desire to resume a mother's authority over an obstinate child. 'Your fate, your children's, mine and that of us all depends on you alone. The time for arguing is past, my dear son, nothing you can say to me could make me change my opinion. I only ask this last consolation from the tenderness you have always shown me. Campi will tell you he has left me ill in bed; your last letter has contributed in no small degree, just as your obstinacy will probably contribute to shortening my days. You can bring me back to life and happiness. Have you the heart to refuse? It's the last time I shall ask you.'

This was the period of the Austrian wedding, which was celebrated at the Louvre* on April 1; Kings and princes were cooling their heels at Compiègne, but Napoleon found time to grant an interview to Campi, who had arrived bringing Lucien's latest 'offer' – he would accept a non-hereditary post, failing which he asked for passports for the United States.

* In the Salon Carré, changed into a Chapel.

'He's raving,' the Emperor complained. 'It's all over . . . Please tell my relations I want to hear no more about this affair.'

The rupture was complete. Lucien was busy with preparations for departure to the New World; he asked arrogantly to have Lolotte back, then suddenly gave way to rage and lost control of himself when he realised that he had lost a battle which he should have avoided. He laid the blame on his mother: 'I am writing this letter to insist on my daughter's return; I demand it by the right I have to do so, and if some wretches tell you you should oppose me in this, they are making you commit an injustice and behave badly to me as a mother . . . Send back my daughter if you love me and if you wish to avoid a scandal . . . My greatest grief at my departure is leaving you, but it has to be, since the Emperor has abandoned all justice towards me, and since you yourself have sided with the others and forgotten the language of honour and religion towards me . . . If the family had done their duty and been less cowardly I should have been reconciled with my brother, but they have always foolishly compared my marriage to Jerome's, and now they are comparing my divorce to the Emperor's.'

Madame Mère and Napoleon were to see Lolotte leave for Italy with sighs of relief. Firmly indoctrinated by her father before leaving Canino, the girl had shown 'mistrust of friendship and presents'; she wrote very bitterly about all she had seen and heard at Court, making fun of the Imperial Family and even gibing at Madame Mère's stinginess – Madame Mère, her own grandmother, who had dreamed of making her an empress!

Thus the greatest diplomatic scheme of Madame Letizia's 'reign' ended in fiasco.

* * *

The marriage of Napoleon and Marie-Antoinette's great-niece, a Habsburg descended from Charles V and Louis XIV and therefore connected with the most distinguished lineage in Europe including the Bourbons, was naturally an occasion to display all the power and splendour possessed by the Imperial Court. The Queens of Spain, Holland and Westphalia, the Princesses Elisa and Pauline – green with rage it must be admitted – carried the train of the new Empress, whose dazzling youth and bloom were set off by a dress of silver-embroidered tulle, while her forehead was encircled by a diamond crown. Napoleon wore a cloak, coat and breeches of white satin and a cap glistening with precious stones on his head. Madame Mère followed them, walking confidently and with the majestic gait suitable to an empress whose children ruled half Europe.

'My mother-in-law is a very amiable and much respected princess,' wrote Marie-Louise to her father; my sisters-in-law are extremely agreeable; the vice-reine is very pretty.' Courtly phrases, intended to be read by her husband, the family and ambassadors, but at heart this young woman brought up in fear and horror of the 'Corsican' had little sympathy for her sisters-in-law – Caroline was too domineering, Elisa too cantankerous, Pauline too pretty, while her mother-in-law inspired her with inexplicable terror. The lack of sympathy and impossibility of communication were mutual, and Madame Mère had already made the often repeated remark: 'She's not one of us.' The ice would never be broken and for four years the two women observed each other with frozen politeness. Besides, at the moment Madame Mère had new family problems, taking precedence over all other considerations, for it was now Louis's turn to draw the Emperor's thunder upon himself.

To avoid meeting his wife when he returned to Paris in December 1809 for the divorce proceedings, the King of Holland put up at the Hôtel de Brienne with his Minister for Foreign Affairs, seven officers, three stewards, three cooks, five valets and six footmen, and proceeded to keep Madame Mère up to date in the story of his troubles; from their very first meetings at the Tuileries, Napoleon had gone into the attack.

'Holland is nothing but an English colony, and more hostile

to France than England herself ... I want to swallow up Holland.'*

A few days later he informed Louis that he ought to abdicate, and Louis wrote to his ministers in Amsterdam; 'Pity your country, but also pity my strange and cruel fate.' As if to make his case worse, Louis suddenly insisted on a separation from Queen Hortense, not even appreciating the fact that having sacrificed Josephine, Napoleon had to protect the Beauharnais children. The family council rejected the request and by Imperial decree Hortense was authorised to live in Paris, her husband being obliged to pay her a pension of a million francs a year and leave her the custody of her children. A few days later the King was forbidden to return to Holland.

'It is my desire that you abdicate,' Napoleon explained. 'Become a French prince again.'

'You can make me give up the throne,' Louis protested, 'I have no way of preventing it; but when I am no longer King of Holland, you can never force me to remain a French prince.'†

From that day the Hôtel de Brienne was placed under police supervision, and Madame Mère had to see gendarmes watching the exits and controlling the comings and goings of *povero Luigi*, who fell ill with a nervous fever just at the moment when his capital was on the point of being occupied by French troops and he was to be forced to negotiate. One morning Madame Mère heard very familiar sounds: cheering in the street, followed by a rapid step on the stairs. Napoleon burst into Louis' room, where he was lying wrapped in blankets and with his bedside table crowded with medicine bottles.

'So you are ill, you're in a bad mood. You must cheer up, go out and amuse yourself. I'm going hunting myself!'‡

---

* On the occasion of Louis Bonaparte's audience at the Tuileries in December 1809, in the presence of Fontanes, *Grand Maître* of the University.

† Conversation between Napoleon and Louis at the Tuileries in January 1810, reported by Roëll, Dutch Minister for Foreign Affairs.

‡ F. Masson: *Napoléon et sa famille*.

Not a word about politics, for the fate of Holland had already been settled: it would either be made a sort of prefecture of France by treaty, or else it would quite simply be annexed, the tyrannous action being disguised by bantering brotherly friendliness and sweetened by a concession.

'All political considerations require that I join Holland to France . . . but I see that is such a painful thought to you that, for the first time, I am bending my policy to my desire to please you . . . I hope what has happened may serve as a lesson for the future!'*

So Louis returned to his States, but not for very long, and Madame Mère's house was calm again, some twelve days after the crushing wedding ceremony: she added up her accounts, for although, like some maternal ant, she had charged Louis with two-thirds of the expenses of her Household during his stay, she was appalled at the cost. To recover from the blow, and the exhaustion of the celebrations, she decided to go and take the waters at Aix-la-Chapelle; a piece of news, or a mere rumour, was enough to hasten her departure: after having refused her a further increase of her dower, it was quite likely that the Emperor would insist on her giving a reception in honour of the new Empress. She set off without a moment's delay – with two of her ladies, a gentleman-in-waiting, a doctor, her secretary, several Corsicans and Pauline – but with a troubled heart, because the quarrel between Nabulio and Louis had broken out again more violently than before, and an explosion of some sort was to be expected.

'Do you want to play an honest part in politics?' Nabulio asked his brother. 'Love France, love my glory . . . Be a Frenchman and the Emperor's brother first, and rest assured that by so doing you will further the true interests of Holland. But what is all this fuss about? The die is cast, you are incorrigible.'†

On June 28, Louis was in fact informed that French troops would enter Amsterdam on July 4, to see that the 'treaty' was

---

* F. Masson: *Napoléon et sa famille*.
† Ibid.

'Her Imperial Highness'

respected, and that he must organise celebrations that day, to show Europe the excellent relations between the two countries.

'I won't be present at the celebrations,' he protested. 'I shall cease to reign on July 4.'*

Madame Mère was told what followed, during her stay at Aix-la-Chapelle. The King had proposed to abdicate, and as his ministers accepted his suggestion, he left the royal palace by a secret door during the night of July 1–2, with three officers and his old dog. On the 9th Holland was reunited to France by a decree that had been prepared on the 3rd. Like everyone else, Madame Mère read in *Le Moniteur* the account of the arrival in Paris of the Crown Prince of Holland, Louis' son.

'Come, my son,' the Emperor told him. 'I will be your father, you won't lose anything. Your father's behaviour has grieved me to the heart. Only ill health can explain it. When you are a man you will pay his debt and your own.'†

A separation between the King and Queen Hortense was declared, all *povero Luigi*'s possessions were confiscated, and Nabulio put the seal on his dealings with this much-loved brother with a lapidary phrase:

'The King has been embittered by a chronic illness that left him no peace for four years, irritating and exasperating him so that he was no longer fit for his job.'‡

For some days Madame Mère was devoured by anxiety and distress, for no one knew where the King had taken refuge from the Emperor's anger: some thought he had embarked for the United States or England, or joined Jerome in Westphalia.

'No one understands what he's up to,' exclaimed Nabulio – and that bodes no good at all!'

On July 20 it was at last learned that the King was not at a spa, as he should have been, but at Toeplitz within the Emperor of Austria's realm. Madame Mère received a furious note from

---

* F. Masson: *Napoléon et sa famille*.
† D. Labarre de Raillicourt in *Le Moniteur*.
‡ F. Masson: *Napoléon et sa famille*.

Nabulio: 'His entire behaviour is inexplicable, and can only be attributed to illness.' This was not the opinion of the interested party, who wrote to his mother in his turn a few days later: 'After all that has happened I have chosen this place as being as far away as possible. I seriously thought of coming to join you, but I should have made you sad, and at present I can only stand the most complete retirement. I am waiting for the Emperor's reply telling me where he will let me stay after taking the waters. I don't know where to go myself; what I would like best is to live with you as a private person in the South of France, but the Emperor wouldn't allow it; then I asked to stay in Germany. I await the Emperor's reply.'

Another delicate negotiation for Madame Mère to undertake. 'I will not leave you all alone,' she wrote to *povero Luigi*; 'however it seems to me that after taking the waters you ought to do what I suggest, that is to come to St. Leu or Pont, where I will go and wait for you and we could decide what is the best thing to do.'* Napoleon didn't treat the fugitive so gently, and wrote saying that his place was in France, and that he must be there by December 1 'under pain of being held disobedient to the Constitution of the Empire and the head of the family, and treated as such', to which Louis replied briefly: 'I am no longer a French prince.'

As if the air were not full enough of threats and dangers, news now came that Lucien, having embarked for the United States in August 1810, had been captured by a British warship and taken to Plymouth as a prisoner of war. 'Ever since you left,' his mother wrote to him, 'tears and grief have been my lot. Everything I dreaded most has now happened . . . I shall have no peace of mind, nor possibility of it, until I get news of you . . . If life still has any value for me it is only because I hope to see you again some day.' Alas, she would not see him until 1814, in Rome, after Nabulio's abdication. As for Louis, although she intervened to get him a passport 'enabling him to go anywhere he liked, from

* The château of St. Leu-la-Forêt, confiscated from the Duc d'Orleans during the Revolution, had cost Louis 600,000 francs in the early days of the Empire.

the south of France to Italy', he preferred to settle in Gratz, where he was to stay until 1813, when Austria (who had granted him hospitality) was at war with France.

'Must I put up with such outrageous behaviour from someone I have treated like a father,' said Napoleon almost in tears. 'I brought him up on the feeble resources of my pay as a lieutenant in the artillery: I shared my bread and the mattress on my bed with him ... And where does he go? Among foreigners, to make people think that he isn't safe in France.'*

* * *

On March 20, 1811, Paris was awaiting the most important event of the reign, to be greeted by a salute of twenty-one guns if the child was a girl, and a hundred-and-one if it were a boy, the hope of the dynasty. The twenty-second report announced the birth of the King of Rome, and by aerial telegraph and couriers galloping night and day, all Europe got the news. 'Never had the birth of a prince produced greater rapture in a nation and more effect in the world at large,' as the Emperor remembered at St. Helena.

'Now the finest part of my reign is beginning,' he declared that day.

The Emperor of Austria was to be godfather and Madame Mère the godmother; she it was who handed the child to Napoleon, who lifted it in his arms to receive the acclamations of kings, princes, high officers of State and a crowd estimated at more than three hundred thousand persons.

'I envy him,' Napoleon confided to one of his faithful friends. 'Glory is awaiting him, whereas I have had to pursue it ... He only has to put out his arms and take the world.'

At the banquet provided by the city of Paris, Madame Mère sat on her son's right, but as she was not in a mood of rejoicing she did not appear at the State dinner at the Tuileries, nor the outdoor festivities at St. Cloud which brought the celebrations

* F. Masson: *Napoléon et sa Famille.*

to an end, but preferred to return to Aix-la-Chapelle, where Pauline was to join her. From there she would go to Westphalia to see Jerome – Jerome who was in great need of solid support to help him resist Napoleon's desire to divest him of Hanover.

But her stay at the famous spa was a dismal one, interrupted by quarrels with the extravagant Pauline (who was distributing gratuities and presents with both hands) and spoilt also by bad weather. After the celebrations of St. Napoleon, on August 15, including a ball at the prefecture attended by her Household and the inauguration of a 'rue Napoléon', Madame Mère began her journey. What a joy to find Jerome, with the charming manners of someone brought up at Court, exerting all his ingenuity to give his mother pleasure: he had sent to Paris for furniture like that of the Hôtel de Brienne, and lighting that wouldn't tire the old lady's eyes, and one of his ministers went to meet her at the Westphalian frontier and escort her to the royal palace, where Jerome and Catherine threw themselves into her arms in front of the entire Court. Fêtes followed each other in quick succession: there were military reviews, hunts, nocturnal performances and masked balls, as if trying to forget the threat hanging over them and the regrets of *povero Girolamo* for a kingdom which appeared to be doomed.

The whirl of pleasure lasted more than a month, until October 6, on which date Madame Mère started her return journey to Paris, leaving her daughter-in-law in tears. 'This parting has deeply distressed me,' Queen Catherine wrote in her diary. 'At her age and in the century we live in it is very difficult to foretell when we shall see her again. It has been doubly painful because Madame Mère was such a delightful companion for me. She has a lot of intelligence and many resources. As I am almost always alone, with only myself for company I found her a great comfort. Also a woman often wants to unbosom herself to another.'

While she was at Cassel Madame Mère got into touch with Louis, who at once drew upon her financially, as his affairs were still in confusion, and scarcely had she reached Paris when it was

'Her Imperial Highness'

Lucien's turn to write from his enforced residence at Thorngrove, asking for money. She didn't hesitate, for she was never mean where her own family were concerned. By a channel unknown to the Emperor, bankers' drafts were sent to England addressed to someone described pseudonymously as Mr. Douglas ... A hundred thousand francs – but then she thought better of it, for she knew Mr. Douglas so well ... 'Only pass it on to him on small accounts,' the banker was instructed. 'That will be better. There is some anxiety about his health. Find out what he needs.'

Napoleon was right. What an excellent mother!

* * *

Towards the end of 1811, when Napoleon and Marie-Louise had returned from a journey in Holland, and Napoleon was beginning to lay his plans for the Russian campaign, Madame Mère came seldom to the Tuileries except to see her adored grandson, or for official receptions. It may have been during one of these overpowering evening parties that a scene took place which was described by the gossips of Paris.

Since his marriage to Marie-Louise, the Emperor had imposed the ceremony of hand-kissing, but Madame Mère regularly avoided taking part.

'Am I not the Emperor?' he said crossly, one day.

'And am I not your mother, and after all aren't you my son?'

Nabulio laughed and kissed her hand affectionately, but Marie-Louise was amazed.

'At Vienna, my Mother, I always kissed the Emperor of Austria's hand,' she said.

'There, my daughter, the Emperor of Austria was your father,' Madame Mère replied with some dignity, 'but here the Emperor of France is my son. That's the difference.'*

The difficult year of 1812 had now arrived, 'the beginning of

---

* E. Marco-Saint-Hilaire: *Mémoires d'un Page*.

the end', as Prince de Talleyrand slyly called it. As if the family troubles were not sufficiently testing – with Lucien a prisoner in England, Louis exiled in Bohemia and Joseph in danger in Spain – Nabulio must needs attack Cardinal Fesch savagely for his dealings with the church and its head – an affair whose ins and outs Madame Mère failed to understand, though she instinctively felt it might draw divine wrath on his head.

The Emperor had convoked a council of the prelates of France, Italy and the Confederation of the Rhine, on April 27, 1811, on the pretext of settling the question of the canonical institution of bishops – the Pope having refused investiture to dignitaries chosen by the civil power – but with the hidden purpose of forcing the sovereign pontiff to acknowledge the supremacy of the Empire, and to come and take up his abode in the French capital, as a vassal. However, all these prelates, who didn't turn a hair at celebrating mass before the man excommunicated by Pius VII, suddenly began to display remarkable indocility; it seemed that being cheek and jowl together in the same room had fired them with unaccustomed courage... To control this battalion according to his plans, Napoleon needed a man who had adopted his own views, and had the influence, talent and skill to make them prevail, even imposing them if necessary. But it was Fesch who presided, in his capacity as Cardinal, Archbishop and Primate of Gaul – a man whose knowledge and faith were equally meagre and whose authority over his colleagues was disputed. Being anxious not to appear merely as his nephew's mouthpiece, Madame Mère's brother allowed opinions contrary to those he was supposed to defend to win the day. Once again, the family system had failed the master of the Tuileries.*

And Fesch, who had received the purple from the Emperor, took it into his head to speak of the rights attached to his divine

---

* Napoleon had very little belief in his uncle's theological knowledge.
'Where did you learn all that?' he asked him. 'Wasn't it in Italy, when you were speculating in my soldiers' bread? Let the experts have their say about matters you have never understood.'

mission. In 1812, as on the 18th Brumaire, reactions were violent: three 'contending' bishops were arrested and shut up at Vincennes and then, by making some small concession Napoleon contrived to get the Pope – held prisoner at Savona – to annul his excommunication, and felt himself sufficiently fortified by this victory to compel some prelates to resign, close the seminaries and send the seminarists to join the army ... On March 1, 1812 he turned violently on the Cardinal.

'I don't need your lectures; go back to your diocese and don't leave it again until I tell you.'*

It was a severe blow for Madame Mère, to whom the astute Cardinal wrote before leaving: 'Don't add to your worries by wondering about the reasons for my leaving Paris. I have laid them at the foot of the cross: God will give me strength; I have put all my trust in Him. I shall never regret my stay in a place where I have been unable to do as much good as I would have liked, and where I was subjected to continual torments of every description, even if I deserved such punishments for my obstinacy in remaining outside my diocese for so long, and for daring to believe I was of use to the Church.'

In May, Napoleon left to take command of the army and march against the Tsar, who had sent him an ultimatum. On his way he gave orders for the Pope to be transferred to Fontainebleau – now that he had been terrorised by the measures taken against the clergy he would be better disposed when the Imperial armies returned from Russia in triumph.

'1813 will see us in Moscow,' Napoleon repeated, 'and 1814 in St. Petersburg. The Russian war will be a three years war.'

He wrote very confidently to Marie-Louise: 'I have been making war for nineteen years, fought countless battles and undertaken countless sieges in Europe, Asia and Africa. I shall hurry up and finish off this one so as to see you again soon.' Madame Mère was not given to a similar optimism and she was not afraid to predict to Nabulio:

* F. Masson: *Napoléon et sa famille.*

'I should be very much surprised if God didn't give you some harsh lesson.'

She had left Paris for her château at Pont, crushed by the loss of her secretary, the Baron Guieu, who wrote such good letters, was *au courant* with all her troubles over Louis and Lucien, and understood her moralising ways and her schemes for economising. To replace him, the Empress Marie-Louise herself had recommended young Elie Decazes, a thirty-two-year-old lawyer, whose greatest talent was to please everyone, particularly Queen Hortense and King Louis whose adviser he had been, encouraging them to resist Napoleon when he annexed Holland.* With the arrival of summer the question of visiting a spa naturally arose, and Fesch suggested Aix-en-Savoie in his diocese, adding that he would accompany his sister if the Emperor sent him permission from the heart of Russia . . . Excellent diplomat that he was, he also offered to be responsible for all the expenses, which was one way of forcing Madame Mère's hand.

In July, while Napoleon was occupying Minsk and marching on Vitebsk and Smolensk, Madame and Pauline were back at Aix, soon to be joined there by the Queen of Spain, and then the Cardinal with a large retinue of carriages, horses, silver, pots and pans, wines and servants . . . The visit was not a great success in spite of the happy reunion. Pauline bored everyone to death with her parties and receptions, her troupes of actors, handsome men and doctors – for she was a perpetual invalid – and the Cardinal suddenly found the waters disagreed with him seriously, as they were 'too strong, if not even dangerously exciting, for a man of sanguine temperament'.

On August 23, Madame packed her bags and returned to Paris, where Marie-Louise, who was sick of being alone at the Tuileries

* Elie Decazes (1780–1860). After the Empire he pursued a career that had begun well: prefect, chief of Police in 1815, Minister of the Interior, President of the Cabinet, he was finally created *duc et pair* by Louis XVIII, who loved him more than a father and who appointed him French Ambassador to London when he was forced to leave politics by a cabal. Decazes founded Decazeville with its important ironworks. The art of pleasing leads anywhere.

without Napoleon to organise the whirl of receptions, came to pay a visit to 'her dear Mama', as she called her.

'I've come to ask you to give me dinner, Madame ... but please don't go to any trouble. I'm not here as the Empress ... I've come to pay you a private visit.'

'Good heavens,' interrupted Madame Mère, drawing her towards her and kissing her on the forehead. 'I won't stand on ceremony either ... I will receive you as my daughter ... and the Emperor's wife shall dine with the Emperor's mother.'*

She paid a brief visit to Pont and then returned to Paris on October 27 – but it was a Paris rife with bad news. There was also the affair of the Republican general Malet, who attempted to seize power by announcing that the Emperor had been killed: the Chief of Police and the Prefect of Paris foolishly allowed themselves to be arrested, but a few hours later the authorities came to their senses and the rebel was tried and shot, after making a famous remark.

'Had you any accomplices?' he was asked by the president of the Council of War.

'France – and you yourself, if I had been successful.'

The fact remained that none of the faithful gave a thought to the natural heir, the king of Rome. 'The Emperor is dead, long live the Emperor.' No one thought of this logical succession because there was something so fabulous in the very character of the regime, depending entirely on the glory and genius of a single man. Madame Mère wrote to Louis: 'You will have read in the papers the news of the rising, or rather the farce that was played at Paris on the 23rd. I had left ... The unfortunates paid for their folly with their lives and all is calm and peaceful in the capital, as it is in the rest of the Empire.'

A few days earlier, on the 19th, Napoleon had given orders for retreat, and had left Moscow after first setting fire to the Kremlin. On December 10, he entrusted the command of the remains of the Grand Army to Murat, and left Warsaw, and on the night

* Madame d'Abrantès: *Mémoires*.

of 18–19th he arrived at the Tuileries, exhausted but still full of spirit, his face half-covered in a dark beard. Next morning he was at work laying plans for a battle against a united Europe. After giving orders for a levy of 300,000 conscripts, and after planning this campaign that was to be his last hope, he considered the idea of having both the Empress and the King of Rome crowned, with a view to keeping Austria neutral, for she would 'not dare make war on her own kindred', and also to ensure that the throne passed to his son in the event of a bullet or an attempt on his life . . . He therefore had to come to an agreement with the Pope; to the great delight of his mother, otherwise there could be no coronation of mother or child. He went in person to Fontainebleau, and realising that concessions would be desirable Pius VII allowed a new Concordat to be extracted from him. 'The Emperor and Empress are expected back from Fontainebleau either today or tomorrow,' Madame Mère wrote to Elisa. 'I suppose you have already heard of the arrangement with the Pope . . . It's one of the best pieces of news for us to rejoice over. Besides which, it will lead to my having the pleasure of seeing your uncle here. An invitation has already been sent for him to come at once to Fontainebleau with the other cardinals and a certain number of bishops.'

Alas! the period just beginning, from January to mid-April 1813, the date when Napoleon rejoined the army, was to be a testing-time for the mother of kings, whose sadness could not be diminished either by Fesch's return or Louis' moves towards a rapprochement.

Poor Louis! Hearing of the defeats in Russia, he offered his services, on condition that the independence of his beloved Holland be recognised.

'Your idea of the situation is completely wrong,' Nabulio replied. 'I have more than a million men at my disposal, and a sum of two hundred millions in my coffers. Holland will always remain French.'

Then, thinking better of it, and not wanting to drive Louis to make some desperate and spectacular move, he got their mother to write to him: 'The Emperor asked me to read his reply to you. So far as I can judge, apart from the question of Holland, you ought to be satisfied. He ends with a strong request for you to join him in Paris, and I add my entreaties to his, and implore you not to refuse his invitation this time. I beg you in the name of everything you hold most dear and as the greatest proof of your affection you can give me personally. If necessary, I command you, as your mother.' All in vain! 'I would rather suffer a thousand deaths than do something against my conscience, against my duty,' Louis replied. Upon which, the Pope, influenced by the Roman cardinals, refused to sign the Concordat, and Fesch had no alternative but to return to his diocese. So there would be no coronation of Marie-Louise and the little King of Rome, and Madame Mère became a member of a Family Council which merely entrusted the regency to Marie-Louise, a child-wife who was secretly advised by the Arch-Chancellor, Cambacérès, a learned but rigid character with little political sense.

On April 11 Napoleon reviewed his army on the Place du Carrousel. 'There was something superhuman about it,' wrote Balzac, 'it was magic, a simulacrum of divine power, or perhaps the fugitive image of this very fugitive regime.' On the 15th he was on his way to Germany to take part in a fierce campaign against a formidable coalition – Russia, Prussia, Sweden, and soon afterwards Austria; of course there was also financial support from England: 666,660 *livres* to the King of Prussia, 1,333,334 to the Tsar, for the expenses of carrying on the war, as well as 500,000 *livres* to the Emperor of Austria, Marie-Louise's father, so that he should resume hostilities against his son-in-law, 'Buonaparte'!

On May 21 Madame Mère retired to Pont, where she was shortly joined by Queen Catherine; Jerome had sent her to France on the pretext that Westphalia was no longer safe, but in reality to give more time to a new mistress. It was a melancholy time for a young woman accustomed to the fairy-tale existence Napoleon's youngest brother knew so well how to create: it rained without stopping, and Madame Mère wore her sternest expression, for her illusions and her confidence in Nabulio's lucky star were dissolving day by day, like clouds before the wind. Perhaps God's harsh lesson was approaching as she had foretold. 'I shan't go anywhere this year,' she wrote to Elisa in June 1813, 'I'm at Pont . . . Staying here suits my health and my character. I am free and calm, and busy having an English garden made, more to give work to the local inhabitants than in the hope of enjoying my creation myself.' How right she was: in less than a year the beautiful house was set on fire by Nabulio's enemies on their march to Paris, and the pretty English park destroyed. 'We are anxiously awaiting the result of the Emperor of Austria's mediation to bring about the proposed Prague Congress. Pray God it takes place, and also brings us peace.' Yes indeed, for however unbelievable it might seem to his enemies or even his friends, Nabulio had again beaten the Prussians and Russians, and Madame Mère, like everyone else, believed that the Emperor Francis, a sovereign of the 'Family', would offer to mediate and restore general peace – and that it would be a peace favourable to France – whereas the Empress' father had in fact gone over to the enemy, and Napoleon had had a terrible scene with the Austrian Chancellor.

'Well, Metternich, how much did England pay you to turn against me?'

On August 12, Vienna declared war on Paris, and Napoleon scored a point at the very start by once more defeating Blücher at Dresden, and pursuing him with the energy of a twenty-five-year-old general, as he had during the Italian campaign. Would Fortune continue to favour him? No. On her return to Paris at the end of October, Madame Mère heard the news of the ensuing disaster: at Leipzig 250,000 French had fought an enemy army of 600,000 (this was 'the great battle of the Nations') consisting of the joint armies of Blücher, Schwarzenberg, Bennigsen and Bernadotte – that same Bernadotte whom Napoleon had created marshal and a Royal Prince of Sweden. The defeat of the Saxon troops hastened the climax both of the battle and the campaign, and the French armies retired across the Rhine. A few days later Jerome's father-in-law, the King of Würtemberg, deserted the cause of the Great Empire. It was the collapse of a vast dream, the ruin of the family – the clan. And how swiftly it was happening!

The Emperor returned to St. Cloud on November 9, and by the 12th his enemies had reached Dusseldorf. On the 16th the population of Amsterdam rose in rebellion against the French army and welcomed the Russians as liberators. On December 2, the Allies crossed the Rhine in their turn: now the national territory itself was in danger. On his return from Leipzig, Nabulio came to the Hôtel de Brienne to embrace his mother. 'I found him far from crushed, but full of confidence in the success of his plans,' the latter wrote to Pauline ... 'Things aren't as desperate as we thought at first ... The Emperor has left his army safe from the assaults of the enemy, and is exerting all his energy and all his means to prepare to terrorise them once more, if they refuse an honourable peace.'

Family worries were added to these military reverses and political frustrations. Driven out of Spain, but clinging desperately to his royal prerogatives, Joseph – although replaced in his kingdom by Marshal Soult, who would command in the name of the Emperor – was roundly abused by Nabulio, who held him responsible for these reverses and wrote: 'All the follies that have been committed in Spain were the result of my misjudged complaisance towards the King.' Joseph was confined at Mortefontaine under strict incognito, and forbidden to show himself in Paris. Jerome was in much the same case: he had been expelled from Cassel, and Nabulio's instructions were that: 'The best thing under present circumstances is for neither King nor Queen to get themselves talked about. The less they are heard of, the better.' The rulers of Westphalia were therefore lodged in the Palace of Compiègne under the same restrictions as King Joseph. Louis, now a refugee in Switzerland, tried to keep up his blackmailing attitude about Holland, thinking to profit from his brother's reverses to obtain 'restitution' of what he believed to be his kingdom and the re-establishment of his family on the throne. On November 3, 1813, he was at his mother's house at Pont, from where he once more set out his claims. Nabulio flew into a rage. 'I send you a letter from King Louis,' he wrote to Cambacérès, 'which seems to me insane. I suppose he hasn't been in Paris ... If he comes there as King of Holland ... he mustn't be received. He must go on staying incognito with Madame at Pont. Above all the Empress mustn't see him ... It's appalling that he should choose this moment to come and insult me and torment me by forcing me to take drastic measures; it seems to be my fate to be constantly betrayed by the ingratitude of men on whom I have heaped kindnesses, especially by the one for whose education I deprived myself of everything, even the necessities of life, when I was twenty years old.' Full of indignation, Louis packed his bags and left France for Switzerland, then for Lyons (where he lived under the same roof as the Cardinal, and the two men chewed over their grievances together), returning finally to Paris, where he shut himself up in the Hôtel de Brienne wearing the uniform of a Dutch colonel.

In Joseph's case, it was insisted that he should abdicate or renounce the throne of Spain in favour of the Bourbons; but he made difficulties and spoke of compensations, and Madame Mère had to play the ungrateful part of mediator between the two brothers. Negotiations were dragging, and at last Nabulio lost patience and brought the matter to an end with a letter in his most characteristic vein: 'You are no longer King of Spain ... What do you want to do? Will you return as a French prince, and take your place beside the throne? You have my friendship, your appanage, and will be my subject with the rank of prince of the blood ... Haven't you enough good sense for that? Otherwise you must retire to a distance of forty leagues from Paris ... You can live there in peace, while I live. You will be arrested or killed if I die.' To Madame Mère's enormous relief Joseph gave in and offered his brother 'his arm and his advice'. His mother must

'Her Imperial Highness'

have made innumerable journeys between the Hôtel de Brienne and Mortefontaine or Compiègne. As in the darkest and most perilous days of the Paolist insurrection at Ajaccio, she was indefatigable and imperturbable: what mattered was to collect all her family together, and to form the clan into a square, such as was made by Nabulio's National Guard soon afterwards, at Waterloo.

'The time for formalities is past,' she said. 'The Bourbons lost everything because they hadn't learnt to die with their swords in their hands.'

The oracle was speaking through her mouth; it was no time to pick petty quarrels with Nabulio when Spain was lost, Germany and Holland in revolt, and French soil invaded.

On January 1, 1814, Blücher crossed the Rhine, and ten days later Murat, King of Naples, was treating with Austria, and proposing to provide the 30,000 men needed to drive the French out of Italy.

'Murat!' exclaimed Napoleon. 'My brother-in-law, openly betraying me ... I thought he loved me; it's his wife who has made him disloyal – Caroline, my own sister, betraying me!'*

From that day, Madame Mère refused to hear the King of Naples and his wife mentioned. 'She even rejected all advances made by her daughter Caroline, who kept repeating that after all it was not her fault, her voice carried no weight and she couldn't give orders to her husband,' as Napoleon related afterwards at St. Helena. 'But Madame replied like Clytemnestra: "If you couldn't

---

* de Bausset: *Mémoires*. Napoleon had intended that the armies in Italy should march on Vienna, so as to force the Austrian general to break off the battle on French soil and retreat to the Danube, or else to cut the enemies' lines of communications with the help of these same troops. But Eugène took a lot of persuading, and Murat thought only of keeping his kingdom of Naples. Hence his defection. He thought better of it, but too late, and wrote Napoleon an astonishing letter: 'Sire, Your Majesty is in danger. The capital of France is threatened yet I cannot die for you, and Your Majesty's most devoted friend seems like an enemy. Say one word, Sire, and I will sacrifice my family and my subjects; it will be my ruin but I shall have served you.'

give him orders, you ought to have fought him; but what battles did you fight? Did your blood flow? Only across your dead body should your husband have been able to stab your brother, benefactor and master."'

Having appointed Joseph his lieutenant-general and entrusted the regency to Marie-Louise, Napoleon left to join his army on January 25, 1814, and performed further prodigies, waging and winning with the help of eighteen-year-olds, who were popularly known as the 'Marie-Louises', the battles of St. Dizier, Brienne, Champaubert and Montereau.* He had a presentiment that this was the final indulgence to be shown him by Destiny. 'If I should lose a battle or you get news of my death, send the Empress and the King of Rome to Rambouillet,' he wrote to Joseph. 'I would rather my son's throat was cut than see him brought up in Vienna as an Austrian prince ... I've never seen a performance of *Andromaque* without sympathising with the lot of Astyanax in outliving his family, nor thinking it fortunate for him not to survive his father.' As for Madame, Hortense, and Queen Catherine, they could remain in the capital. These detailed orders did not in fact change the course of events, and the little king started on his journey to Austria, where he was to become merely the Duke of Reichstadt, while Madame Mère had to put many miles and a frontier between herself and her son's enemies.

By March 28 everything was over, or nearly. The Tsar looked down at Paris from the hills surrounding Napoleon's capital, and determined to revenge the violation of Moscow. A Council of Regency met at the Tuileries, but though Madame Mère was present she didn't utter a word. Her common sense told her that the testing time had come, and that exile would begin at the very palace gates. It was decided that the Regent and the King of Rome should remain in the besieged city, to frustrate plotters, prevent the Bourbons being proclaimed, and safeguard the future of the

* Under the French monarchy, the rank of lieutenant-general was conferred on a prince of the blood, thus delegating him part of the royal power in time of crisis.

Bust of Madame Mère

Cardinal Fesch

Madame Mère

dynasty. Napoleon II, as emperor under Marie-Louise's regency, would perhaps gain the support of the allied sovereigns, at least that of his grandfather. Joseph then rose and read aloud the Emperor's instructions: 'You must not under any circumstances allow the Empress and the King of Rome to fall into enemy hands ... If he advances on Paris in such strength that any resistance is impossible, the Regent, my son, the high officials of State and the Senate, the presidents of the Council, the officers of the Crown, the Baron de la Bouillerie and the Treasure must all be sent south towards the Loire.'

The Emperor's orders were not questioned. Next day at nine o'clock in the morning, a procession of ten carriages left the palace: in the third were Madame Mère, Jerome and Catherine. They spent the first night at Rambouillet, and the second at Chartres, where they heard that Paris had surrendered.

'At least they put up a good fight?' asked Madame Mère.

'Marshal Moncey was admirable.'

She confided simply to one of the courtiers:

'I shan't complain however it ends, if only Napoleon retires without loss of honour, for falling from power is of no importance if one makes a noble end. It is everything when one makes a cowardly one.'

At eleven o'clock on the 31st, Paris was invested by the enemy armies and the allied sovereigns let it be known that they would not negotiate with 'Napoleon Bonaparte' or any of his family. The fugitives set out for Blois. In the midst of catastrophe Napoleon still found time to think of his family and attempt to organise a retreat which he guessed might be confused, explaining to Joseph on April 2: 'I have written already that Blois must not become congested. The King of Westphalia can go to Britanny or Bourges. I think it would be best for Madame to go and join her daughter at Nice, and Queen Julie and your children to travel towards Marseilles ... King Louis has always loved the Midi, and it is natural for him to go to Montpellier. It is essential to have as few as possible people on the Loire, and that everyone finds lodgings without causing any stir ... Recommend the strictest possible economy to them all.'

On the 7th, like everyone else, Madame Mère heard the official news of the abdication at Fontainebleau but she was unaware of the admirable remark made by this Emperor, who was abandoned by everyone after having bestowed so many kingdoms, principalities and duchies. As he retired from political life, leaving history for legend, he merely advised those negotiating the treaty:

'So long as my family is provided for; that is all that matters to me.'

There would be a million francs a year for Josephine, 400,000 for Eugène, 300,000 for Madame Mère, 500,000 for Joseph, 200,000 for Louis, 500,000 for Jerome and 300,000 each for Pauline and Elisa. What was more, their pride was safeguarded. 'The Emperor's mother, brothers, sisters, nephews and nieces will keep the titles of princes of their family, wherever they reside.' Napoleon and Marie-Louise were to keep their imperial titles.*

On the 8th an envoy from the Tsar arrived at Blois in search of the Empress, whom he was to escort to Rambouillet where the Emperor of Austria was awaiting her. He had written to Napoleon that he was offering his daughter 'the hospitality of his family for several months' ... Vienna was clearly anxious to break with the past as quickly as possible, and must have regretted the existence of a fruit of that troublesome union!

Marie-Louise called on her mother-in-law to say goodbye.

---

* A few days later, on April 20, 1814, Byron foreshadowed the verdict of history in a letter to his future wife, Annabella Milbanke: 'Buonaparte has fallen – I regret it – the restoration of the despicable Bourbons – the triumph of tameness over talent – and the utter wreck of a mind which I thought superior even to Fortune – it has utterly confounded and baffled me – and unfolded more than "was dreamt of in my philosophy". It is said the Empress has refused to follow him – this is not well – men will always fall away from men – but it may generally be observed that no change of Fortune – no degradation of rank or even character will detach a woman who has truly loved' (*Letters and Journals*).

'I hope, Madame, that you will continue to think of me as kindly, as you have been good enough to do hitherto.'

Madame Mère looked her straight in the eyes.

'That will depend on you, Madame, and on your future conduct.'

VI

'The Corsican Niobe'

'In the Name of the Emperor and King, we, Baron, Mayor of Orléans, Officer of the Legion of Honour, invite the civil and military authorities to allow Madame, mother of the Emperor and King, native of Ajaccio, *département* of Corsica, now resident in Paris and travelling with her suite, to pass freely without let or hindrance from Orléans, *département* of the Loiret, to Nice and Genoa, *départements* of the Alpes-Maritimes and of Genoa, and to give her such assistance and protection as may be necessary.

Issued at Orléans, April 9, 1814
For the Mayor of Orléans, his deputy
Dufaur D. Pibru
Cost of passport: Two francs

Age:	64	Mouth: small
Height:	5 feet	Chin: rounded
Hair:	turning grey	Face: oval
Forehead:	rounded	Complexion: clear
Eyebrows:	brown	Special peculiarities: none
Eyes:	brown	
Nose:	well shaped	

Signature: MADAME

1793–1814 ... So eleven years had passed since she arrived at Toulon with her seamstress passport, destined (along with her family) to live through one of the most astonishing dramas of history. Only eleven years, but lived at a tempo imposed by Nabulio, in other words, at full tilt. Once again she was a wanderer, with her two franc passport, but this time with the astonishing eminence of being: 'the mother of the Emperor and King', the mother of one of the greatest men of all time, and provided with a privy purse of 500,000 francs for her journey, given her by the Regent according to instructions from Nabulio, who always thought of everything.

She was joined by the Cardinal, who had left Lyons to avoid falling into the hands of the Austrians, and they travelled together by short stages, through Roanne, Lyons and the Mont-Cenis, along the road to exile, under the protection or supervision – impossible to say which – of a colonel of the gendarmerie. They stopped for a week in the Corrèze, to give the Cardinal time to send instructions to Paris and Lyons to put his private business in order; then at Lyons itself, where the man who still thought of himself as the Primate of Gaul hoped soon to return, and devote himself 'entirely and exclusively to his diocese'. On April 27 the Austrian commander himself, the Prince of Hesse-Homburg, came to give them safe-conducts and offer them an escort. At Casena they met Pope Pius VII leaving his prison at Fontainebleau, but he made himself very amiable and promised them hospitality in his States or even in Rome, which, as he subtly emphasised, 'had always been the home of important exiles'.

And so, on May 14, rather like someone waking in a familiar room after a dream, Madame again found herself in the Falconieri Palace in the Via Giulia, which she had left in 1804 to go to Paris for the Coronation. 'Here I am in Rome with Madame, who is pretty well in spite of the exhaustion of a very long journey, made more disagreeable by the circumstances and a troubled mind,' the Cardinal wrote to Queen Caroline. 'But we have arrived, and time will cure all.'

In every situation, this brother and sister showed a very rare practical good sense: hardly had the Cardinal got down from his carriage, when he took steps to have his possessions registered in

Corsica in the name of a cousin of his, and to sell his house in Paris, thus preserving them from possible confiscation; while Madame Mère made arrangements to transfer her Hôtel de Brienne and acquire a *palazzo* or *palazzotto* in Rome. Most conveniently, Louis XVIII's government was looking for an official residence for the Minister for War, and the mother of the Emperor and King remembered her bourgeois prudence and was not above haggling over the price ... Financial dealings and even threats did not dismay her. 'I paid much more for my house than the price our expert put on it,' she wrote to her lawyer. 'I do not want to sell it. However, as the government is asking for it and wants to buy it at a price fixed by the experts, I agree to sacrifice it; but I insist that the valuation should follow the rules and not the whim of any individual ... If they abuse their position you must solemnly protest on my behalf.' The royal government offered 600,000 francs, but Madame insisted on 800,000 and refused to discuss the matter, even when it was suggested that she might well 'repent' of her intransigence. In the end she won her price, keeping for herself the large quantity of sumptuous furnishings – too expensive for the buyers of the house – and having it packed up and sent partly to Rome and partly to Elba with calm assurance. Next she got rid of the ruins of her château at Pont for the sum of 100,000 francs, cheerfully erasing from her mind her memories of a village she had been much attached to, but which had rallied to Louis XVIII with such enthusiasm that it was now called Pont-le-Roi.

She was about to prepare for her journey to the island of Elba, planning as usual to join the one of her children who was in greatest trouble, when chance provided her with the immense happiness, among so many trials, of being reunited with Lucien, who brought his enforced stay in England to an end, and whose chief concern it must be said was to shower attentions on the Pope, in order to prove what an abyss now separated him from 'the iron hand', as he now called Napoleon. At last, in June, the letter she had been impatiently awaiting arrived. It was from

General Bertrand, the Grand Marshal of the Palace, and it contained 'orders'. 'The Emperor will be delighted to see you on the Isle of Elba and has prepared rooms for you. If Your Highness is to sail either from Civita-Vecchia or Leghorn, the Emperor will send a brig to fetch you and bring you here. It is a fine brig and very suitable.'

An Officer of the Royal Navy, in command of the frigate *Curaçao* offered to take her to Porto-Ferrajo, and she was about to accept and set off, when the British Commissioner of Elba, Colonel Neil Campbell, opposed the plan, as 'the Navy does not allow passengers to be carried on board His Majesty's ships, without regular orders and permission from superior authorities'. In the end, with Campbell's consent, she made the voyage from Leghorn to Porto-Ferrajo on board the brig *Grasshopper* on August 2, with a suite consisting of her chamberlain Simeon Colonna, former prefect of a province of Naples, two ladies (Mesdames Blachier and de Blou), old Saveria, and a chaplain, the Abbé Buonavita.*

Colonel Neil Campbell, who kept a Diary, describes these negotiations and the crossing made by the traveller with the discreet pseudonym of Madame Dupont, whom he calls 'the old lady'.

'July 31st. Visited Madame Mère in company with Captain Battersby, of H.M.S. *Grasshopper*. She got up as if with difficulty, some seconds after our approach, and made us sit down upon chairs close to her ... I addressed her as Madame and Altesse; she was very pleasant and quite unaffected. The old lady is very handsome, of middle size and with a good figure and fresh colour ... After remaining for half an hour we bowed and went off. Madame Mère will sail tomorrow or next day and I intend to accompany her ...

'August 2nd. Embarked in H.M. brig *Grasshopper*, Captain Battersby, with Madame Letizia, Mr Colonna and two dames

---

* The Abbé Buonavita was later sent by Madame Mère to be Napoleon's chaplain on St. Helena.

d'honneur, and landed at Elba the same evening. In leaving the inn at Leghorn to walk to the boat Mr Colonna took the arm of Madame, with his hat off all the way. Captain Battersby and myself took the arms of the two ladies with our hats on. Captain Battersby and two of his officers, M. Saveria a passenger and myself all dined with Madame upon deck. A couch was arranged for her, from which she never stirred during the whole voyage, except once to look out for Napoleon's house, when she mounted upon the top of a gun.'*

Napoleon was not at Porto-Ferrajo that day, as he had been staying in his country house, the hermitage of Marciana, for several weeks. When he was told during dinner that his mother had arrived, he at once embarked in his cutter, which was sheltering in a neighbouring little port, and although the sea was rough, he sped towards his 'capital', where he arrived soon after the brig had dropped anchor. When she saw him, after these four taxing months, Madame wept tears of joy, which were soon dried when she found herself greeted with spontaneous cheers by an exuberant crowd of little people who reminded her very much of the inhabitants of Ajaccio, and above all when she was sitting next to Nabulio in his carriage.

Napoleon's valet Marchand noted that she looked very well, was still beautiful, and held herself erect in spite of her sixty years, 'appearing ten years younger than she really was'. Saveria seemed very old and deaf, but still ruled the Household with a firm hand and the most ferocious parsimony. She was anxious to see Nabulio...

'Well, my good Saveria,' he said teasingly, 'are you still just as mean as ever?'

The sly creature had learned a thing or two from her mistress; she muttered:

'It's not meanness, Sire, it's foresight.'

Madame and her Household were to occupy the Casa Vantini, close to Mulini (where Napoleon was installed), one of the

* Neil Campbell's *Napoleon at Fontainebleau and Elba*, 1864.

prettiest houses in the little town, rented for two hundred francs a month. It wasn't the Hôtel de Brienne nor yet the château of Pont, but more like the Casa Bonaparte at Ajaccio, and Madame Mère was enchanted. 'The Emperor has got ready a charming house beside his own. We go out every evening in the carriage or garden,' she wrote to Lucien. 'He has had a large terrace made, with a view over the sea. At night we play reversi. There's plenty of company.' It was a simple life; the drawing-room hangings were faded and the carpets worn in places; the lanes were crowded with donkeys and redolent of fried fish and olive oil, but on all sides one heard the gay tones of people speaking Italian. How good it would be to live here, after so many disappointments and worries – including the exhaustion of being great and powerful!

Court life had never been to her taste, and she had been separated from her son for ten years by the barriers of etiquette and successive military campaigns, so that Madame was delighted to find the Mulini 'palace' only a hundred yards from the Casa Vantini, and the Emperor apparently resigned to a bourgeois existence so that his family could enjoy his company; and she told herself that this transformed royalty of the isle of Elba would after all allow her to return to the roles of mother and mistress of a house, the only ones she really enjoyed. Every evening she climbed the steps of the road leading to Mulini, to dine and play reversi, which she had looked forward to all day while doing embroidery and chattering with her ladies. Oh, of course everything didn't always turn out as she would have liked. Nabulio hadn't changed, he was just as impatient, just as eager to win, cheating scandalously. There were some evenings when poor Madame fidgeted in her chair, pursed her lips and sponged her forehead.

'Napoleon, you haven't reckoned it right . . . I assure you!'

'You're rich, Madame, you can afford to lose; I'm poor – I have to win.'*

* Pons de l'Hérault: *Souvenirs et anecdotes d l'île de Elbe.*

He laughed at her protests, got up, pocketed the handsome gold coins with his effigy on them, and returned to his own rooms with his booty. Next day he would sometimes give way to her complaints and agree to 'review' the score and pay back his illicit gains. Sometimes he read his mother the lampoons which came pouring in, and tried to get her to share his own amusement at their outrageousness.

Later, at St. Helena, he recalled:

'When they told me, or I read, that I was a strangler, poisoner and rapist, that I had had the sick massacred, or drove my carriage over my own wounded soldiers, I could only laugh in pity. How often I said to Madame: "Come, Mother, and look at the savage, the tiger-man, the devourer of the human race; come and admire the fruit of your womb".'*

The old lady put up with his teasing, for he overwhelmed her with kindnesses, inviting her punctually every evening to drive along the sea-shore in his calash, constantly concerned with her material comforts, her health, her rank; presenting all the island officials to her and insisting that they attended her Levée on Sundays at the Casa Vantini. Thus it was that Madame made friends with Rosa Mellini, the charming daughter of an officer in the Engineers, and took her on as lady-in-waiting and then secretary. Rosa went with her to Rome and signed her letters for her when age and infirmity prevented her doing it herself.

With the first hot days – and they were crushing – Nabulio took refuge in his hermitage, and organised a visit there from his mother with that minute attention to detail which characterised all he did. 'I've brought my three iron bedsteads,' he wrote to the Grand Marshal. 'My orders are that one should be taken to Marciana for Madame Mère. She'll be comfortable in the adjutant's house ... There will be a room for her and three for her suite. The large pieces of necessary furniture are already in the house. I'll add a chest of drawers. I think there are enough kitchen utensils, candles and lamps. Send three curtains for her room. The

* Las Cases: *Mémorial de Sainte-Hélène.*

'The Corsican Niobe'

rods are there already. Send us fireplaces, shovels and tongs. I think they're right when they say one needs a fire in the evenings.'

Madame obeyed all these instructions, so reminiscent of those given to armies or the commissariat, without a murmur and with a kind of automatism which struck all who saw it. She was the mother of the Emperor and the mother of Nabulio, and that meant that she had witnessed a career which had astounded the world, as well as a difficult and stormy childhood, but all the same Napoleon found it hard to communicate with her: stiff, often silent, nearly always sitting motionless on her chair, she seemed to have been turned to stone by time and troubles, perhaps tired of playing the role for which she had been cast, and dazed, like someone waking from a dream and letting herself be guided mechanically between reality and unreality. Perhaps she simply regretted her own economy of words and gestures, and felt short of ideas in comparison to her rather frightening genius of a son, or was sorry not to have more taste for parties which were the Mulini household's only way of escaping boredom, in short not to measure up to the standards of the very unusual person with whom she spent her days.

Pauline arrived, most welcomely, at the end of October, and took over responsibility for the entertainments, clubs, dinners, concerts, masked balls and theatrical performances of the Court and the island as a whole, thus saving Madame all the drudgery involved, and leaving her only the duties of presiding at the family dinner on Sunday and putting in an appearance at the evening assembly.

Napoleon on the isle of Elba was Gulliver among the Lilliputians. His capacity for work was so great, his eye for detail so pitiless that he had to tackle everything, even though during his first days there he had said lightly:

'The island of rest. Henceforth I should like to live here like a justice of the peace.'*

* To the Austrian general, Koller. (J. A. von Helfert: *Napoleon I-Fahrt von Fontainbleau nach Elba.*)

He appointed a governor, a steward and a treasurer-paymaster-general, he instituted a court of appeal, reorganised the customs office, the octroi, the police and the gendarmerie, made a general plan of the road system, built a hospital and a theatre, modernised the fortifications, reinforced the batteries and enlarged the barracks. And the inevitable happened: the expense of all this work and these festivities, and the support of the 1,200 soldiers who had chosen to follow their Emperor, rapidly became too heavy a burden for his slender funds to bear, and by the end of 1814 only two of the four millions he had brought from France remained to him. There was no question of reducing expenses and leading the life of a recluse, any more than of disbanding his little army, for fear of exposing himself to some surprise move from the Royalists – who were occupying Corsica and were said to be planning to kidnap if not assassinate him – or from the Barbary corsairs who infested that part of the Mediterranean.

Madame offered him all her jewels – which Napoleon refused – and then a contribution of 500,000 piastres, but this was not enough to fill the ever-increasing hole in the funds of a Household which had kept its extravagant tastes, and in the spring of 1815 the exile saw that he might be compelled to try and reconquer his Empire... Everything inclined him to the same conclusion, even invited him. At the Congress of Vienna, some had proposed that it would be better to transport him by force to the Azores, St. Lucia, the Cape Verde Islands or St. Helena. He could only defend himself from such an abuse of strength by keeping his Old Guard and maintaining his fortifications in good order, and that could only be done with the help of the subsidies guaranteed by the Allied sovereigns, of which the King of France did not pay his share. The decision to take to the sea was therefore more or less suggested, or even imposed on him by his enemies: it was almost as if some subtle, twisted mind had plotted to lead him into this ambush of History, and, when Colonel Campbell suddenly went away for twelve days in the spring of 1815, he seemed to be obeying mysterious orders.

Madame Mère has left us her impressions of these decisive days in her *Souvenirs*: 'One evening the Emperor seemed to me more cheerful than usual; he invited me and Pauline to join him in a game of écarté. A moment later he left us and shut himself up in his study. As he didn't return, I went to call him, and the chamberlain told me he had gone down into the garden. I remember that it was one of the sweetest spring evenings; the moon was shining among the trees, and the Emperor was alone, striding rapidly up and down the garden paths. Suddenly he stopped, and leaning his head against a fig-tree exclaimed:

"All the same I must tell my mother about it."

'At these words I went to him and said very impatiently:

"Why, what's the matter with you this evening? I see you're much more preoccupied than usual."

'After a moment's hesitation, he put his hand to his forehead and answered:

"Yes, I must tell you, but I forbid you to repeat what I'm about to confide, to anyone at all, even to Pauline."

'Then he smiled, embraced me, and went on:

"Well, I want to warn you that I'm leaving."

"Where are you going?"

"To Paris. But above all I want to ask what you think of the idea."

"Ah, then you must let me try and forget that I'm your mother, just for a moment."

'I thought for a little and then said:

"Heaven will not let you die by poison nor in unworthy inactivity in this forgotten island – but sword in hand . . . Yes, go, my son, and fulfil your destiny."'

Thus speak Corneille's heroines, so greatly admired by Napoleon, even when the heroism of those they love destroys their domestic happiness.

* * *

On Sunday, February 26, the day of his departure, Napoleon dined with Madame and Pauline and then received the most important men of Elba before he authorised those who were to share his perilous adventure to come and kiss the hands of his sister and mother. Through her tears Pauline explained to Marchand, Napoleon's head valet, that the case she was slipping into his hand contained a diamond necklace, and that if the Emperor should meet with misfortunes this jewel, estimated to be worth half a million francs, might come in useful to him.

'Goodbye,' she sobbed.

'I have every hope that it will only be au revoir, Your Highness,' murmured the young man.

'I cannot think the same.'*

It was true that she would never see her brother again. Madame had also given way to her emotions and was in tears.

'I trust my son to you ... Here,' she said giving Marchand a bonbonnière with her portrait painted on the lid, 'see that he uses this one in future instead of the one he has now; and if fortune goes against him don't desert him.'

She hid her face in her hands and wept uncontrollably: however her prayer was heard, for Marchand remained faithful to his master, and was one of those who watched by the Emperor's deathbed on St. Helena.

As night fell, the two women stood on the terrace of the Mulini, watching the flotilla carrying Caesar and his fortune as it disappeared from view: seven small ships crowded with nearly a thousand men. The Emperor had ordered them to go to Rome, and thence to Paris if his landing should be successful. Full of confidence in the outcome, Madame Mère hastened to communicate the good news to Lucien. 'I shall leave in three days time, weather permitting. The Emperor has departed with all his men, but I do not know where he has gone.' Two days later Colonel Campbell returned and upbraided Pauline in round soldierly terms.

* L. Marchand: *Mémoires*.

'The Corsican Niobe'

'Your brother has broken his parole; he promised never to leave the island; but the Mediterranean is full of ships, and he'll be a prisoner by now.'

Prompt as he was to stigmatise Napoleon's breach of parole, the Colonel never uttered a word about the Allies' refusal to carry out their obligations as laid down by the Treaty of April 11, 1814, nor about the difficulties into which this had plunged the sovereign of Elba.

'That's no way to talk to a lady!' Pauline said indignantly.

But this delicate and beautiful young woman was in such mortal terror of being arrested, that two days later she fled on a small boat with two or three others – which gives some idea of the fear the Colonel's threats had aroused in her. Madame, for her part, faced the situation boldly, altered none of her habits, and when a courier announced the success of the desperate but glorious adventure, she shared her joy with *caro Luciano*. 'I have great pleasure in giving you the news of our dear Emperor's departure from this town and of his arrival in Golfe Jouan (sic) near Antibes ... His lucky star has saved him from all danger and fear ... The local inhabitants received the Emperor with joy. Couriers were sent to all departments to announce the day of resurrection ... Our Emperor will have been received with open arms by all the troops and the French people. On March 1, the Emperor set off at midnight for Lyons.'*

With the eagle and colours flying from steeple to steeple as far as the towers of Notre-Dame, the Emperor was soon carried into

---

* This bold and successful attempt amazed Byron, who wrote to his friend Thomas Moore on March 27, 1815: 'Making every allowance for talent and the most consummate daring, there is after all, a good deal in luck or destiny. He might have been stopped by our frigates – or wrecked in the Gulf of Lyons, which is particularly tempestuous – or – a thousand things. But he is certainly Fortune's favourite, and

> Once fairly set out on his party of pleasure
> Taking towns at his liking and crowns at his leisure,
> From Elba to Lyons and Paris he goes,
> Making *balls for* the ladies, and *bows to* his foes.'
>   (Byron's Letters and Journals.)

the Tuileries by a crowd intoxicated with wild delight ... Madame Mère hadn't the patience to wait for the promised ship: she embarked with all her suite at the beginning of April, on the *Joaquim* and the *Caroline*, both of them sent by the Queen of Naples. At Portici she met the Cardinal, just arrived from Rome; when he heard of Nabulio's departure from Elba he had exclaimed: 'My nephew is crazy'; also Jerome, who had escaped from ferocious Austrian surveillance at Trieste, and lastly Queen Julie. They sailed up the coast to Gaeta, to await the *Dryade* which was to take them to France, but were forced to be patient as she was chased by a frigate and a brig of the Royal Navy. Not till the 13th did they set sail, only to fall in with the enemy and have to put in at Bastia in their native isle of Corsica. They had left it twenty years earlier, and were never to see it again.

The governor came on board to greet his illustrious guests and escort them on shore. 'All Bastia was collected there, and the civil authorities and the few remaining military leaders were drawn up on the quay in fine array. A gun was fired.' Madame leant on the governor's arm, the Cardinal beside her, King Jerome a little ahead. They passed under arches of greenery set up in haste, Madame responding graciously to the cheers of her fellow-countrymen. For two hours she gave audience to persons of importance, then as the look-out signalled that the enemy sails had vanished she hastily reembarked, leaving the ladies of Bastia disappointed of the evening party they had begun to organise.

On May 22 the *Dryade* dropped anchor at Golfe-Juan, at the very place where Napoleon had landed two and a half months earlier. They spent the night at Antibes where they were received with due respect, and then set off for Paris by the valley of the Rhone, arriving there on June 2, as the Cardinal wanted to make a stop at Lyons in his beloved diocese.

'As soon as the Emperor heard that Madame had arrived in Paris, he got into his carriage and went to see her, finding his brothers there as well,' wrote Marchand. 'It was a long time since Madame's heart had felt such sweet delight as this family reunion

Letizia Ramolino-Bonaparte

Madame Mère's death mask

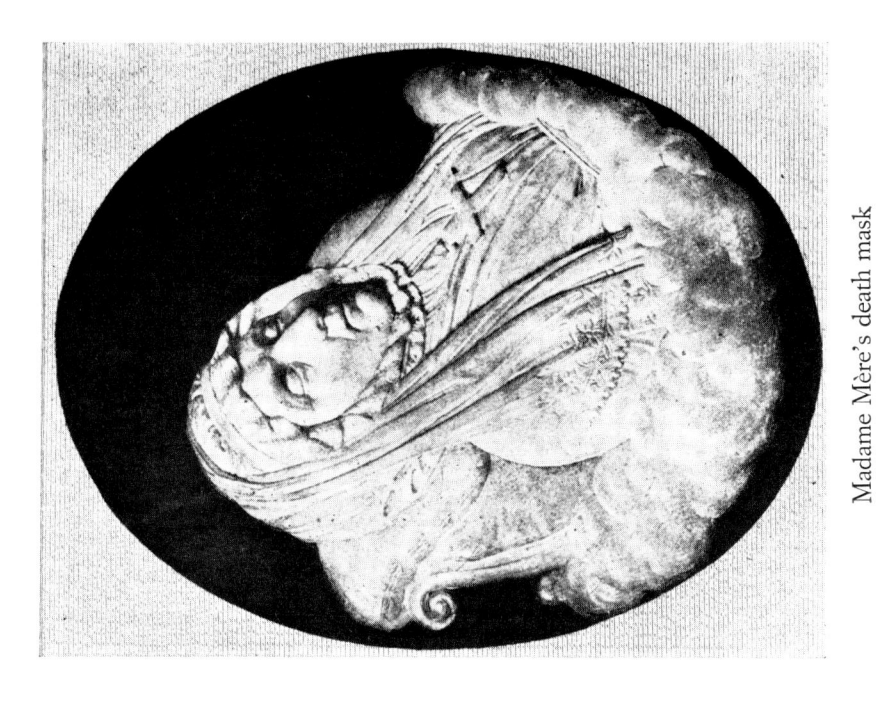

Madame Mère in her old age, drawn by her grand-daughter, Charlotte

gave her.' Four of her sons were now in the capital – Napoleon, Joseph, Lucien and Jerome; since Lucien's rapprochement with 'the iron hand' in the moment of danger he was addressed as His Imperial Highness Prince Lucien, established in the Palais Royal, received the ribbon of a Grand Officer of the Legion of Honour and always wore the uniform of a colonel of the National Guard.

On June 7, Madame was present at the ceremony of the opening of the Chambers, and heard Nabulio speak sternly to the assembled members:

'A formidable coalition of kings has designs on our independence ... You, peers and representatives alike, will give the Nation an example, by your confidence, energy and patriotism ... The army and I will do our duty.'

She had lost none of her astounding majesty of demeanour, despite the humiliating interlude on the island of Elba, and her presence drew the gaze of everyone. 'At about four o'clock a door was heard opening, and all eyes turned towards a gallery decorated in honour of Madame Mère and Queen Hortense, followed by their ladies-in-waiting,' wrote Mademoiselle Cochelet, reader to Queen Hortense. 'The Emperor's mother must have been one of the most beautiful women in the world. In spite of her age, one was still struck by her regular features and the air of nobility in her whole person. I remember that she was wearing a high-necked lace gown, with long sleeves lined with orange satin, a small hat trimmed with white feathers and magnificent diamonds, as was her dress. Her beautiful black eyes with their long lashes and delicately arched brows could still rival those of many young women in brilliance and expression.'

On Sunday June 11, Madame must have attended the last mass in the Tuileries, and noticed sadly – as others did – the change in her son's appearance. 'His gaze, once so formidably searching, had lost its power and even its fixity ... His mouth was contracted, and lacked its former charm ... Everything about him seemed unnatural and discomposed; his usual pallor had given way to a distinctly greenish tint.' After the family dinner, the Emperor left the Elysée, and took the road northwards to Belgium – to Waterloo, one of the most important confrontations in the whole of history, dozing in his travelling coach like some Greek hero hastening towards disaster with a sort of determination. As he took leave of the assembled court, he called out to the Grand Marshal's wife:

'Well, Madame Bertrand, let us hope we won't regret the island of Elba!'

In another five days the drama was over. On the morning of June 21 he was back at the Elysée, not having had his boots off once since the 17th, the eve of the battle which he would have won had his plans been carried out, if he had not provoked Fate once too often, if his enemies had not learned their lesson. He was dropping with sleep and exhaustion, and threw himself on a divan like a sleepwalker, while one of his valets pulled off the boots that were heavy with the mud of the battlefield.

Next day he abdicated for the second time, and should also have started making plans to escape from the vengeance of Blücher, who was threatening to have him hanged, and of the royalists who longed to assassinate him. However, he had never been outwardly calmer, and maintained a vague confidence in his star, repeating that 'his destiny must be carried out'. After a conversation with Madame Mère, Josephine's daughter, Queen Hortense, knocked on the door of his study and spoke to him in simple and sensible terms:

'Sire, don't think of yourself alone ... If you choose America, make haste to get to the port before the English hear what is happening. If Austria, make your conditions at once; perhaps their sovereign will remember that you are his son-in-law. As for the English, it would be too great a triumph for them, and they would imprison you in the Tower of London.'

When the time came for a final decision which should not tarnish his image, he took refuge at Malmaison, haunted by memories of Josephine – the place where his career had first taken shape. Here he decided to go to the United States, and here he awaited news of the two frigates promised him by the new French government. 'You will have heard of the Emperor's latest misfortune, and that he has just abdicated in favour of his son,' wrote Lucien to Pauline. 'He is going to leave for the United States of America, where we shall all join him. He is full of calm courage. I shall try and join my family in Rome and take them with me to America. If your health permits, we shall meet again there.' Shut in that strange library, suggesting a crypt with its arches supported on pillars, and in which he had conceived the great designs of the Consulate, he looked through some books about the New World and received his faithful followers – or rather the last of his faithful followers – and his business advisers. The Grand Marshal's wife, who was Irish on her father's side but English in taste, tirelessly repeated that he ought to seek refuge in England, and that the free and enlightened English were the only race worthy to receive him and capable of understanding him.

He allowed his followers to lose precious time by collecting furniture, a library, silver, just as if he wanted to leave it to chance to settle the crisis for him. Why didn't he jump into his carriage and drive towards a port, without pausing to draw breath? Had he embarked before the British navy could mobilise its strength, he would have reached America without difficulty. But his anxiety to leave the political scene with dignity may have turned him against this project of a furtive retreat to a distant country. Perhaps he dreamed of falling under enemy blows like Caesar, or perhaps he wished to be the only famous man to die buried alive beneath his great deeds on a lonely rock. Unless . . . His doctor had given him a flask containing a brown liquid. He handed it to his valet saying:

'See that I have this somewhere on my person, either in my jacket or some other part of my clothes, but so that I can get at it quickly.'*

The Prussians were approaching Paris and they would not take him alive.

Then news came that the frigates were in readiness at Rochefort.

* L. Marchand: *Mémoires*.

It was June 29, and he decided to leave at once, after he had taken leave of his family.

'Madame Mère was the last member of the imperial family to come and say goodbye to the Emperor,' wrote the famous actor, Talma. 'What a noble and tragic occasion I witnessed . . . What a scene it was, this separation between mother and son! Although she extracted no sign of emotion from the Emperor, she inspired the eloquence of his fine features, his bearing, and no doubt also his thoughts . . . Madame Mère's own feelings were shown by the two large tears that rolled down that fine classic face, and only three words came from her lips when she stretched out her hand to him as he left:

"Farewell, my son!"

'The Emperor's reply was equally brief:

"Mother, farewell!"

Then they embraced. Thus took place a separation that was to prove eternal.'

He left by the door leading into the park, and threw himself into a carriage which disappeared among the foliage: he was on the way to Rochefort and further troubles, in a state of indifference, almost as if he already knew that his enemies had kept in reserve for him that apotheosis he had dreamed of.

He was to say later at St. Helena: 'Adversity was what my career lacked. If I had died on the throne, amidst the clouds of my omnipotence, I should have remained a problem for many men; today, thanks to misfortune, they can judge me naked as I am.'

* * *

'Your mother will stay with me in France until her children have reached whatever destination Providence guides them to,' the Cardinal wrote to Pauline on June 28. This destination depended less on Providence than on the four Ministers for Foreign Affairs of Austria, Great Britain, Prussia and Russia, who met on August 27 and decided, among other things, that Lucien, who could be sure of the Pope's hospitality in his capacity as Prince of Canino, a pontifical title, could retire to Rome along with Madame Mère and his brother, but 'the Court of Rome will be invited in the name of the Allies to take responsibility for the Prince and Princess of Canino and the other members of the family, and while consenting that they be given shelter, they insist in the most positive terms that they be kept under constant supervision'.

Installed in her Hôtel de Brienne, Madame Mère was still cherishing the insane hope that the Allies and King Louis XVIII would authorise her and some of the family as well to go on living in France – her brother for one, for he had taken possession of his museum residence again, Joseph's wife (no longer Queen Julie but Madame Joseph Bonaparte) and Josephine's daughter (no longer Queen Hortense but Madame de Saint-Leu). After all, she liked to remember, Napoleon had shown clemency towards certain members of the Bourbon family, and even come to their assistance. But the royalists would not listen to anything of the sort, and were infuriated by this reminder: 'Their effrontery is unbelievable,' wrote a lady of the old nobility.* 'For instance, Madame, Bonaparte's mother, actually says that since Madame la Duchesse d'Orléans remained in France, she can do so too. It's unbelievable. Are people going to put up with this sort of thing?' They didn't put up with it, and Louis XVIII, who had been playing at being an easy-going monarch, was less tolerant than the man they called a tyrant.

Forgetful of his dignity, the Cardinal went even further: on July 10 he wrote to the King parading his difficulties – his sister's illness, the problems of his diocese (from which he had effaced the 'ravages of the Revolution'), and of his financial situation. He received short shrift, most fortunately for his reputation and Madame Mère's, for people liked to think she was involved, though she knew nothing of the affair. Through the intervention of the Chief of Police, the King simply sent passports for Rome.

* Madame du Cayla.

Fesch was indignant, declared that he was being plundered, announced that he wouldn't leave France while his property was sequestered, dared to maintain that he had received 'neither favours nor perquisites', and accused the sovereign of wanting to force him to undertake a long journey into exile 'in a manner far from suitable to his dignity and almost denuded of resources'. They should at once pay him the arrears of his endowment as First Chaplain of France, of his pensions as senator and cardinal, and salary as archbishop and Grand Officer of the Legion of Honour. Beneath the purple worn by this prince of the church there still existed the soul of the little clerk in the commissariat of the Italian army! He was told bleakly that he must first obey His Majesty's orders and leave France, and Fesch at last made up his mind to pack up his pictures and books and transact the fictitious sale of his house in Paris.

Poor Madame, seemingly forgotten by her former secretary and protégé Elie Decazes – who owed everything to the imperial family and had been made prefect of police before becoming a favourite of the King's – poor Madame packed her trunks, sold her furniture and adopted a disdainful and indifferent attitude when they tried to frighten her by spreading rumours that she was to be arrested. At last, on June 22, the *Journal de Paris* published the paragraph her enemies were expecting: 'The day before yesterday, Madame Letizia Fesch, the widow Buonaparte, left Paris. A uniformed officer and another in plain clothes were in her carriage. She only took with her a valet and a lady's-maid.' Prince Metternich had provided the Austrian escort, and in fact Madame was accompanied by her chamberlain, Colonna, and a lady-in-waiting, while the Cardinal took a secretary with him.

The following Sunday they were at Bourg, and Fesch celebrated High Mass surrounded by his clergy in his beloved diocese, which he would never see again. On the 25th they arrived at Geneva, and pressed on as far as Sècheron to visit Queen Hortense, and Prangins to rest in King Joseph's empty château, where their Austrian escort came to say goodbye.

'Captain,' said Madame Mère, 'in spite of your sovereigns' relentless hostility to the Emperor Napoleon, I am prouder of being his mother than I would be if I were the mother of the Emperor of Russia, your Emperor and all the kings in the world.'

Queen Hortense saw her go sorrowfully, because misfortune had brought her closer to this woman of whose almost hostile coldness she had once been afraid. 'The Genevan authorities forced her to continue her journey,' she wrote, 'without letting her rest for a day and without any consideration for her great age and her misfortunes.' Yet this region of Switzerland had welcomed young General Bonaparte, when in 1797 he had led his army along the Lake of Geneva towards the Valais, to organise the crossing of the St. Bernard, swoop down on the plains of Italy and win the battle of Marengo. 'How everything changes in this world!' as Chateaubriand used often to comment.

By July 13 they had reached Bologna and Fesch requested the Grand Duke of Tuscany's leave to stay in his States. This prince, Ferdinand III, was Marie-Louise's uncle and brother to the Emperor of Austria; he had danced attendance on Napoleon at the Tuileries to solicit support or even a smile from the Emperor, and was proud of having been prince-elector of Wurzburg in the Confederation of the Rhine. But he was only one of those fickle friends of Fortune, and he replied harshly that after a restorative rest the old lady and the Cardinal could 'find it convenient to continue their journey'. So they set off once more, having lost a few more illusions concerning crowned heads, and reached the Falconieri Palace in Rome on the morning of August 15, supported by Pius VII, who, to the annoyance of most of the cardinals, promised them that 'If Madame Letizia and Cardinal Fesch arrive under no restraint the Holy Father will raise no objection; if they arrive under surveillance he will receive them all the same.'

Napoleon was a good judge of character and when at St. Helena he said of the Pope:

'He's a kind, gentle, excellent man – a lamb, an influence for good.'

VII

'The Mother of all Sorrows'

The refugees were still travelling along the roads of France when an ultra-royalist deputy, the Comte de Corbière, proposed a legal project to the Nation's representatives: 'The ancestors and descendants of Napoleon Buonaparte, his uncles and aunts, nephews and nieces, brothers, their wives and children, his sisters and their husbands are excluded from the Kingdom in perpetuity, and are directed to leave it within a month, under pain of the punishment detailed in article 91 of the Penal Code. They can enjoy no civil rights there, nor possess any property, titles, or pensions freely granted to them, and they are directed to sell property of every description within the next six months, subject to payment.' It was a serious threat, for Article 91 mentioned 'death and confiscation of property'. But in political matters 'exclusion in perpetuity' is often short-lived, and as the Comte de Corbière lived to a great age, until 1853 in fact, he had time to see the Second Empire and the installation at the Tuileries of Napoleon III, one of the 'nephews' envisaged by his projected law of proscription. Thus do Empires come and go, but thus also do vindictive calculations come to nothing.

Now that her native land was forbidden, would Madame ever again see all those children who had once worn crowns and were now being hounded from one country to another? Joseph, who called himself the Comte de Survilliers, succeeded where Napoleon failed: he was in the United States where he was building himself a house at Point Breeze near Philadelphia, 'which was going to be the finest after the President's in Washington'. Jerome was at the Court of his father-in-law, the King of Würtemberg, living a life not unlike a prisoner's. Elisa was at Trieste, Caroline in Austria, but Pauline, Lucien and Louis were fortunately at Rome. As for Nabulio, he was sailing towards his island-prison, where he would land about the middle of October: henceforth he would be the unhappiest of her children, and it was on his behalf, and towards the improvement of his lot, his comfort and preservation, that Madame Mère now devoted all her efforts and resources.

For the present she had to set up house in this strange city of Rome, where administrative tasks were carried on by all ranks of ecclesiastics. 'They were judges, advocates, professors, notaries, writers, custodians of museums and libraries,' said Stendhal derisively. Heaven only knew, and the Police and their victims also, how efficient they were! Madame and her friends couldn't move a step or receive a visit without being watched. Another person who kept her under observation was Louis XVIII's ambassador, a bishop, Monseigneur de Pressigny, who flew to his writing-desk as soon as he heard that these dangerous 'individuals' had arrived. 'Cardinal Fesch arrived with his sister last Monday; he is living peacefully in Rome where he has been one of the chief mischief-makers for the last six weeks.' Count Consalvi, the Pope's Secretary of State, had also to be reckoned with, for he felt a most unchristian hatred towards all the Bonapartes. He came to see Madame and questioned her with the rude insistence of a policeman about the current rumour that she was sending large sums of gold to Corsica, to foment some sort of rising.

'Monsieur le Cardinal,' the old lady replied dryly. 'I am not a millionaire... But kindly tell the Pope, so that what I say may be reported to King Louis XVIII, that if I were fortunate enough to own this wealth so charitably attributed to me, I should not use it to stir up trouble in Corsica, nor yet to obtain supporters for my son in France – he has enough already; it would be to arm ships and entrust them with the special mission of rescuing the Emperor from St. Helena, where he is held prisoner through a most infamous breach of faith.'*

The angry members of the Vatican did not calm down till they heard to their stupefaction that the Holy Father had received Cardinal Fesch, and that – incredible though it seemed – he had gone in person to the Falconieri Palace to visit Madame Mère.

* * *

The treatment inflicted on the Emperor, for which all historians hold the British Cabinet responsible – with the result of tarnishing their reputation for ever – was defined by the Prime Minister, Lord Liverpool, and the Foreign Secretary, Lord Castlereagh. Lord Bathurst, Secretary of State for War and the Colonies, issued the orders, and they were carried out by the sinister Hudson Lowe, whose name has been execrated by many for the last century and a half. The behaviour of the governor of St. Helena towards the most illustrious exile in history, and a soldier, aroused the indignation of more than one generous soul. Byron wrote from Venice to his friend Hobhouse: 'There is a long manifesto in the papers of Napoleon against that bugger Hudson Lowe – who treats him more like an officer (Sheriff's) than a Gentleman.' The rules worked out sub rosa by the two ministers – because police searches are hardly the business of a gentleman – were carried out with relish by the heartless governor, eager to make a name for himself and only too willing to act as representative for the Allied sovereigns and the conscience of liberated Europe.

To his gaoler's great fury, the Emperor never failed to remark that he had fallen into the hands of the victorious enemy in violation of the law of nations, by means of infamous stratagems and disregard of the rules of hospitality, and that consequently he

* F. Masson: *Napoléon et sa famille.*

refused to admit to being a prisoner of war. Among other measures enforcing surveillance, he had been forbidden to write or receive sealed letters, it was therefore the task of a lieutenant-general to go so far as to search the baskets of dirty linen leaving Longwood House, and to read and have copied all letters, however harmless, such as those of an old lady to her son deported to an inaccessible island six thousand kilometres away. This was enough to make Napoleon refuse to write in his own hand to any of his family, even his mother, for six years, and it gave him very little pleasure to receive their letters, after they had been opened, read and stamped by his guards. Besides, it was not until May – when he had been seven months on the rock – that he had the joy of recognising a familiar handwriting on an envelope, when the scene described by Las Cases occurred: 'The Grand Marshal handed me a letter for the Emperor, a letter from Europe. I gave it to him: he read it through once, and sighed. Then he read it again, tore it up and threw it under the table; it had arrived opened... He returned to the newspapers he was reading, and then after several moments, looked up and said: "It's from poor Madame; she's well and wants to come and join me" ... and he went back to his reading. This letter, the first the Emperor had received concerning his family, was written in Cardinal Fesch's hand, and the Emperor was obviously wounded to receive it open.' Thanks to the copy made by Hudson Lowe we know the text: 'I am very old,' wrote Madame Mère, 'to make a journey of two thousand leagues; perhaps I might die on the way, but what matter, I should be nearer you.'

At Rome itself they only got news of St. Helena from Mrs. Skelton, wife of the lieutenant-governor, who had been living at Longwood House and welcomed the Emperor there in October 1815, inviting him to lunch. She and her husband had had the privilege of being admitted to the intimacy of the man who had taken over their little country house, and when they left the island in May 1816 the lady had received a Sèvres cup as a present. As soon as she arrived in Europe she wrote to Madame Mère, and it seems that, in spite of the governor's threats, she brought in her luggage a letter from Las Cases to Cardinal Fesch. 'You cannot imagine the pleasure your letter brought me,' wrote Madame's brother. 'It's the first time we have had news from Longwood. This letter assures us that he was well on May 13. Has he had any news from us? Is it possible to get some to him? Would you be so extremely kind as to send us any you may receive from St. Helena. Could you let us know what we could send him that might be pleasant to him and by what channel, books or anything else.'

It is difficult to understand why in addition to the constraints of exile, affliction and impotence, the warder of St. Helena had conceived the diabolical idea of depriving his victim of maternal comfort and affection.

* * *

In the austere Falconieri Palace every day brought its troubles, and poor Madame trembled with fear when a letter was brought her on a salver, by a valet standing stiffly in his handsome livery of imperial green, or when the Cardinal stopped hanging his thirty thousand pictures, and arrived in a hurry to communicate some news or rumour. One day it was the death of Murat, shot by the Calabrians, after falling into a trap laid for him by his enemies; another day it was Louis, who had become infatuated with a sixteen-year-old marquise and was trying to get his marriage to Josephine's daughter annulled; or else it might be Jerome complaining of poverty and asking for money to buy a château in Moravia or Trieste; or Lucien, whose financial situation was often precarious, since he too was quite incapable of resisting his fancies, and kept buying pictures, land, villas and palaces, only to sell them at a loss at the end of a year.

'My children have never been able to understand as I have, how profoundly humbled we have been by the Emperor's departure,' sighed Madame Mère. 'In happier times I was always open-handed to my children but I have no right to squander my fortune now. No one must forget that I'm ready to do without everything, should the son to whom I owe everything have need of my help.'*

Only Pauline contributed a little gaiety, for in spite of her worries, which she passed off as misfortunes, her position was a good one: separated from the husband she had been married to for so short a while, she had been given a pension and rooms in the palace and the Villa Borghese; afterwards she bought and decorated most charmingly the Villa Paolina – today the Villa Bonaparte and residence of the French Ambassador to the Holy See – haunted still by her gracious ghost.

Detailed and precise news about the odious treatment inflicted on the Emperor by Sir Hudson Lowe, in contempt of the generous traditions of British hospitality, had an effect on public opinion at the beginning of 1817, thanks to the devotion of a Corsican servant who had been chosen to go to St. Helena out of charity.

At the end of 1816, both so as to reduce expenses and out of hope that by creating a void round the prisoner he might be more easily controlled, Lord Bathurst gave orders for an officer and three servants from Longwood (including a certain Natale Santini) to be expelled from the island. Corsican fidelity, based on *esprit de clan*, is not a legend! Santini had been a drummer-boy at fourteen, afterwards an infantryman, and taken part in every battle between 1804 to 1812 under the orders of the 'god of War', who was his god also; he made the journey to the isle of Elba in 1814 at his own expense. This blind devotion pleaded in his favour when the hour for choice came and the Emperor drew up the list of those who would share the terrible 'hospitality' of the *Bellerophon* with him. At Longwood he had proved himself a man of many tasks – including hairdresser and shoemaker – but also a rough taciturn character, all of one piece, whose daily dream was to kill his master's gaoler.

* Madame Mère to Elisa Bonaparte.

'What's this, you brigand; you want to kill the governor? If you get any more such notions, you wretch, you'll see how I'll treat you,' cried Napoleon when he heard about this obsession.*
But it was to Santini that he confided his desire to protest to all Europe against the barbarous system Hudson Lowe had instituted in the island. And it was Santini who took the text – not in his pockets which the governor's sbirros searched, after stripping him stark naked – but sewn into his waistcoat, copied on a piece of white satin, and even more surprising – a prodigy of zeal for an illiterate – committed to memory. He learned the text by heart in two days, and recited it without a mistake to Napoleon, who smiled, pinched his ears and exclaimed:

'With your air of not knowing how to do anything, I'm pretty sure you'll succeed . . . If you can get to London, have it printed. You'll find there are some fine fellows in London; there are plenty who don't share their government's prejudices against me. Go and find them, they'll help you.'†

The little Corsican set about his task so patiently that with the help of three Frenchmen living in London he drafted a pamphlet which ran through seven editions in ten days. He spoke so well that he was received by Lord Holland, one of the heads of the Liberal party, who called on Lord Bathurst to preserve the reputation of Parliament and the country from the stain it would receive, if Napoleon Buonaparte were treated harshly and without generosity. The Secretary of State got out of this scrape by means of oratory, and treated Santini with condescension, as a man who could not be credited. He expanded the theme of the 'excellent' climate of St. Helena, and of the quality of the wines supplied, and insisted that no member of the family had sent the Ministry any letters for the general. The sly fox! 'Bathurst,' writes Lord Rosebery, 'was one of those strange children of our political system who fill the most dazzling offices with the most complete obscurity.' This question naturally created a great stir

---

* Santini: *De Sainte-Hélène aux Invalides* (1853).
† also L. Marchard: *Mémoires* and O. H. Aubry: *Sainte-Hélène*.

'The Mother of all Sorrows'

through all Europe and troubled more than one conscience; Madame Mère hastened to write to Lord Holland to establish the truth:

'Napoleon's mother can best show her gratitude for the interest you take in her son by expressing her surprise, on reading Lord Bathurst's reply to the effect that none of the family had sent the British minister any letters for St. Helena. Such effrontery confirms the impression your question must have made, and the good results it could have for the Emperor.

'I have written to my son several times, sometimes through commercial channels, among others through the banker Torlonia, who assured me that my letters had been received in the offices, several times also through English noblemen, who graciously consented to hand them to ministers: but I only remember the name of one of them, Lord Lucan, who promised my brother and myself that our letters would be put into the hands of Lord Castlereagh by his eldest daughter, to whom he would send them on arrival in Paris. And since the new year I have sent other letters to General Matthew . . .

'However, Providence, ever watchful to unveil falsehoods, allowed a lady (who was in Rome last February and was said to be close to an Under-Secretary of State – she was called Hamilton, unless I mistake) to tell commander Tower that she had read my letters to my son, that they had been brought to her country house in England. Since the ministers make such use of them, and in the extreme unlikelihood of the Emperor's having received any of my letters, I have decided not to give the ministers cause for amusement so often, even if it means a mother giving up hope of communicating with her unfortunate son.'

A witness heard her murmur, perhaps as she signed this letter:

'I would rather my son thought me dead, than that he doubted my tenderness, or the part I take about his plight, and my hopes of seeing him again.'*

When Joseph suggested her joining him in the United States

---

* Madame Mère to Lord Holland, March 1, 1817.

she explained to Nabulio: 'I can't decide to ask for passports for America. I should have news of you less often.'* The Emperor was right, what an excellent mother!

The man whose glory had ship-wrecked him on an inhospitable isle thousands of kilometres away from his family and his men of affairs, was suddenly threatened with being put on rations if he didn't share the expenses of his own detention. It's the story of the hanged man paying for the cord before his execution, and the Secretary of State wasn't lacking in practical sense. Napoleon replied with a famous phrase:

'If I'm hungry,' he said to Lowe, waving his hand towards the English camp, 'these brave soldiers will have pity on me; I shall go and sit at the table of the grenadiers and I'm sure they won't repulse the first – the oldest soldier in Europe.'†

Like the good housewife she was, Madame Mère preferred action to recrimination, and she made it her business to come to the help of the little colony of exiles. She at once shut her purse to all beggars, even good Princess Catherine.

'At the present moment you must surely know that one of our family is in great trouble, and needs my help more than any of the rest, so that he can have the means of providing himself with necessities, and also pleasant distractions. Everything now belongs to the Emperor, from whom I received everything,' she said. 'When I've nothing left, I'll go begging for Napoleon's mother.'

This simple woman also had her wit, and her son would have liked that.

As the whole family had profited from Nabulio's rise to power, the entire clan must sacrifice themselves at the moment of truth, and Madame didn't mince her words: 'It isn't for me to fix how much my children should contribute towards their brother's needs. My children possess honour, feelings, heart; and all of them should have more means and goodwill to give than is

* Lowe Papers, Volume 20120 (unpublished).
† Las Cas, *Memorial*, Aug. 18, 1816.

'The Mother of all Sorrows'

needed. I shall begin to form a fund by sending 30,000 francs to M. de Las Cases. Let everyone address to him. As for me, I'm ready to give my last sou to the Emperor.'

She sent 65,000 francs to the former chamberlain of Longwood, now the exiles' treasurer; Joseph sent 25,000, Eugène 21,000 and Jerome 15,000 francs. The others, nothing! Not even Fesch, who owed everything to his nephew but who got his sister to write: 'As for the Cardinal, I know how he's situated; he has nothing; he does what he can to keep up appearances, but he has nothing.' Nothing, yet he put it about that he was selling his collection of pictures. Only a Court could pay the price. Nothing, yet he advised Las Cases: 'Write to my sister for everything that could soften the Emperor's appalling fate; she will give all she can.' What a good apostle!

And then Napoleon suddenly decided to use the funds he had placed on deposit with Prince Eugène, about 800,000 francs, and Las Cases would return all the contributions except Madame Mère's, which would serve in cases of urgent need (for instance when Prince Eugène's men of business mistakenly issued a protest against a bill); the Emperor's mother also took over the cost of sending books, clothes, wine and coffee out to St. Helena. The prisoner's parcel!

* * *

In April 1818, Madame Mère bought the Rinuccini Palace on the Piazza Venezia at the corner of the Corso, a *palazotto* built in 1660 and consisting of three storeys and a terrace. She occupied the first floor, visitors and her children or grandchildren the second, and the servants the third. Sober but elegant décor, a hall with paving and mosaics, frescoes, the initials LB surmounted by the Imperial crown, fireplaces designed by Canova, handsome furniture from the Hôtel de Brienne, and above all fine pictures by Gérard, Gros and Isabey, reviving a past that though very recent already belonged to history.

Her way of life was quite dignified: Colonna, the old chamberlain a tall lean figure in court breeches, received the visitors; Rosa Mellini was present and sometimes old Saveria as well, telling anyone who would listen that she had practically been Nabulio's nurse, and handing round bon-bons to the ladies and children. In the mornings Madame went to Mass in one of the churches in her parish, San Lorenzo in Lucina or Santa Maria in Via Lata, and as her carriage went by with the coat of arms on the door, passers-by would call out:

'Napoleon's mother!'

'Well,' she said smiling, 'twenty years ago when I crossed the Carrousel the drums used to beat the honours, and when I arrived the troops presented arms; a crowd used to press round my carriage; now when I show myself people only dare to peep at me through their curtains. Oh well! one sort of interest is as good as another. In the old days it was enthusiasm, today it's politeness... Twenty years ago I was "Your Highness", now I'm "Madame Letizia" again.'

To those who were surprised by the armorial bearings on her carriages, she replied gently but firmly:

'Why should I remove them? All Europe was prostrate before them for ten whole years, and kings had got used to them.'*

Pope Pius VII was enchanted by such firmness: he admired this determined woman who refused to abandon either her dignity or her frankness, and he showed her truly paternal solicitude. Sometimes when driving in the melancholy Roman campagna, sprinkled with ruins and tombs with the eternal light playing over them, his carriage would pass that of the Mother of Kings, and the Sovereign Pontiff would be seen to descend unceremoniously, greet Madame Letizia and walk a few steps with her.

'Have you had any news of our good Emperor?' he would be heard asking.

The old lady's favourite drives were to the Pincio, the Villa Borghese, the Villa Paolina or the Coliseum, whose worn stones

---

* Madame de Sartrouville's *Journal*.

'The Mother of all Sorrows'

enchanted her: perhaps, like Chateaubriand, she listened to the silence and watched her slight shadow slip from portico to portico, and was pleased that the solitude of her last years should have the ruins where the first martyrs died for a décor. She must have thought how insignificant were the things of this world when she contemplated the city from the height of the Pincio, for in what other place have both tyranny and liberty come to grief, leaving only stones piled on stones?

It was in the ruins of Flavian's amphitheatre that she was introduced to Lady Blessington, the beautiful friend of the Comte d'Orsay and Byron. She it was who once answered a surprised visitor's question, in her drawing-room in St. James:

'How sad you seem today Lady Blessington! What's the matter?'

'It's the anniversary of Napoleon's death and I've felt ill all day.'

The woman Byron had called the 'Irish Aspasia' was speechless when confronted with the mother of her idol.

'She is pale and the expression of her countenance is pensive, unless when occasionally lighted up by some observation, when her dark eye glances for a moment with animation, but quickly resumes its melancholy character again; yet even when animated her manner retains its natural dignity and composure, and she seems born to represent the mother of kings. The Prince de Montfort and his excellent wife treat her with a watchful and respectful tenderness; each supported her and suited their pace to her feeble steps, listening with deep attention to her observations. She was dressed in a robe of rich dark grey Levantine silk and a bonnet of the same material worn over a lace cap, with a black blond veil. Her hair was divided *à la Madonna* (her own white hair) showing a high and pale forehead, marked by the furrows of care. A superb Cashmere shawl, that looked like a tribute from some barbaric sovereign, fell gracefully over her shoulders; and completed one of the most interesting pictures I ever beheld. I must not omit recording that her feet are small and finely formed and her hands admirable. Her voice is low, and sweet, with a certain tremulousness in it that denotes a deep sensibility. She spoke of the Emperor Napoleon; and her lips quivered and her eyes filled with tears.

'"I shall soon join him in that better world, where no tears are shed," she said, wiping away those that chased each other down her cheeks ... Sorrow, sanctified by resignation, has given to the countenance of this interesting woman an indescribable charm. The Prince and Princess de Montfort led the conversation to other topics in which Madame Mère joined, but by monosyllables; yet her manner was gracious and gentle, and marked by much of that affectionate earnestness which characterises Italian women, and particularly those of advanced years and elevated rank. When we had made the tour of the garden, walking very slowly in order to avoid fatiguing her she entered her carriage, into which she was assisted by Jerome and my husband; the ex-King and Queen of Westphalia kissed her hand, the latter performing the ceremony with as profound a respect as if a diadem encircled the brows of Letizia, and, that she herself had not borne one. Madame Mère invited us to visit her, and at parting touched my forehead with her lips and shook hands with Lord Blessington, saying kind and flattering things to us both.'*

Several witnesses affirm that Marie-Louise came to Rome with her father in March 1818, and that she got one of her officers to ask whether she could call at the Rinuccini Palace. Madame Mère's reply would have been cutting:

'You insult my daughter-in-law by supposing that she's travelling the high-roads instead of being with her husband, the martyr of St. Helena. The woman you tell me about couldn't be my son's wife, she is a schemer and I don't receive schemers.'

On the other hand the palace doors were always open to those of the French living in Rome who remembered that the Emperor had a mother, and Madame would talk to them at length about her son whose fame had already reached the most distant lands. The wife of a young painter of the Academy of Rome, Clément

* Lady Blessington: *The Idler in Italy*.

'The Mother of all Sorrows'

Boulanger, remarked on the resemblance between mother and son.*

Madame laughed as she said: 'Napoleon had a handsome face when he was in a good humour. When he was considering important affairs his expression grew very serious: then I would say to him: "My child, I shall be cross when people tell me you're like me." That made him laugh and he kissed me. Poor fellow, he was so good! When I said to him, "You work too hard," he never failed to reply, "Was I born with a silver spoon in my mouth?"'

She willingly admitted that Nabulio had made mistakes, even serious mistakes, and sighed:

'Napoleon wasn't infallible. Napoleon wasn't like Jesus, the son of Mary. He was only the son of Letizia. Oh yes, I foretold what would happen, a long time ago!'†

But she was beside herself with rage if anyone called him a tyrant.

'Tyrant, tyrant!' she cried. 'If they had seen him when he was alone, as I have done, they wouldn't call him a tyrant. The Emperor won't be truly understood for the next hundred years.'

Some evenings she dictated to Rosa Mellini her memoirs of her youth and of the rise to power of that naughty child whom, as an old Corsican miller had predicted, would become 'the first man in the world'. And the girl from Elba heard her murmur as if to herself:

'I have never prized honours, nor believed in Court flattery.'

The evenings were passed among these phantoms, or else Rosa Mellini would read some book on the Emperor's life, or his campaigns, but usually the Cardinal arrived bringing some gossip from the town – the Cardinal, who had aged a lot and grown portly, and who began to nod during his own stories.

---

* The resemblance struck Pierre Loti, who wrote in *Le Livre de la pitié et de la mort*, after a visit to the Casa Bonaparte: 'She is like him to look at, she has the same imperious gaze, the same smooth locks of hair; her surprisingly intense expression has in it something sad, haggard and imploring.'

† Madame de Sartrouville's *Journal*.

'Brother!' Madame Mère would say impatiently.
'Yes, Sister?' said Fesch with a start.
'You're asleep!'
'Nothing of the sort ... I was listening to you.'*

When he talked about his own affairs there was no stopping him, and he made mountains out of molehills. In particular, he persisted in considering himself as Archbishop of Lyons and Primate of the Gauls, and resisted with all his strength the intrigues of Louis XVIII's government to deprive him of his See.

'My Church at Lyons is my heritage, my chalice, nothing shall separate me from it. I shall be faithful to it until my last gasp.'†

The Pope was fond of him, and encouraged him to resist; this touched Fesch, who sank into exceptional piety, very different from his former state. He had given up going out into the world, but assiduously attended the papal chapels and the services of the College of Cardinals; he walked barefoot in a procession to the Coliseum, carrying the heavy cross. The brother and sister were so close and intimate that Madame Mère let herself be won over by this religious exaltation and was entirely dominated by a form of mysticism which soon afterwards caused her to fall under the power of an Austrian adventuress claiming to be inspired by heaven.

* * *

Madame Mère spent the second half of 1818 doing her utmost on behalf of Napoleon. When she received a report of his illness from Dr. O'Meara, the doctor at Longwood, she at once showed it to the best specialists in Rome, her own doctor, Dr. Machielli, and four professors from the University. The result of this consultation was sent to St. Helena, but didn't arrive until the middle of 1819, when the invalid's condition was considerably worse. Next, a letter informed her that one of her son's servants had died in February – and been buried by an Anglican in the

* Princess Mathilde: *Souvenirs*.
† Cardinal Fesch to Cardinal Consalvi, June 1816.

'The Mother of all Sorrows'

absence of a Catholic priest – that other members of the Staff were unwell and likely to be repatriated, and that the Emperor was in need of a French or Italian steward who had formerly belonged to his Household or that of one of the family, and a chaplain, 'an educated man under forty years old, and above all gentle, and not full of anti-Gallican principles'.* The Rinuccini Palace was soon buzzing with confabulations: Pauline offered her head cook, Madame her steward (Coursot), who declared simply: 'For the honour of serving the Emperor, I would go to New Holland if necessary,' and the priest who had been her chaplain on the isle of Elba, the Abbé Buonavita. As for the doctor, this was to be Professor Antommarchi, prosector of the School of Medicine at Florence. Well enough for the domestics, who had been well-trained; but an aged abbé, who had had one attack of apoplexy and could hardly speak, accompanied by a certain Abbé Vignali, half priest, half medical student, and a young professor whose medical knowledge was limited to anatomy! They were all Corsicans – that was the secret – and the Cardinal was delighted to be able to declare that their 'zeal' and 'inviolable attachment' could be counted on.

No haste was shown in dispatching this little caravan to the remote island where the invalid was languishing, for it was known that a Congress of European sovereigns was shortly to be held at Aix-la-Chapelle, and Madame Mère cherished the illusion that they would give some thought to the exile of St. Helena. She showed little understanding of these autocrats whom Nabulio had terrorised! Princess Catherine suggested the idea, Las Cases prepared the draft, and on August 29 she signed her 'Appeal'.

'A mother afflicted beyond all description has long hoped that the meeting of Your Imperial and Royal Highnesses would bring her happiness once more.

'It is impossible that the prolonged captivity of the Emperor

---

* The anti-Gallicans were against those who were demanding more freedom from the Vatican for the Church of France, and Napoleon who favoured the Gallicans, did not want an 'anti' as a chaplain.

Napoleon should not be one of the subjects of your discussion, and that your greatness of soul, your power and your memories of past events should not impel Your Imperial and Royal Majesties to deliver a prince who shared your interests and even your friendship.

'Would you leave a sovereign who threw himself on his enemy's mercy, believing in his magnanimity, to perish in the torments of exile? My son could have asked his father-in-law, the Emperor, for asylum; he could have put his faith in the noble character of the Tsar Alexander; he could have taken refuge with His Prussian Majesty, who would surely have remembered his former alliance, had he been appealed to. Could England punish him for the confidence he showed in her?

'... Sires, I am a mother, and my son's life is dearer to me than my own. My sufferings must be my excuse for the liberty I take in addressing this letter to Your Imperial and Royal Majesties.

'Do not ignore this appeal from a mother against the cruelty long practised against her son ... Reasons of State have their limits, and posterity, ever prone to immortalize, reveres the generosity of conquerors above all else.'

They didn't so much as honour her with a reply, and the sovereigns who had so directly sought Napoleon as an ally decided that he was, after all, merely 'the power of the Revolution concentrated in a single individual', and that he was and would remain 'the prisoner of Europe' at St. Helena.

'When I was strong, when I held power in my hands they sought my protection and the honour of an alliance with me, and licked the dust from my boots,' Napoleon exclaimed; 'now that I am old they basely crush me, and snatch my wife and son away from me.'

The Bonapartes should have understood that Nabulio, though doomed to end his days in exile, was in sore need of the help he had asked for, and that the presence of a skilled doctor might ease his pain. Alas! the five individuals they chose so lightly did not start on their journey until the spring of 1819, and this delay

'The Mother of all Sorrows'

would look like indifference had not Pauline thrown a strange light on the state of mind of her mother and uncle at this period.

'I've had much to put up with here these last two years,' she wrote, 'because my uncle, Mama and Colonna have come under the influence of a scheming woman, a German and a spy for the Austrian Court, who says the Madonna appears to her, and told her that the Emperor was no longer at St. Helena! It's all the wildest nonsense! The Cardinal has gone nearly mad on the subject and says openly that the Emperor is no longer there, and that he has had revelations telling him where he is! Louis and I have done all we could during the past two years to destroy the impression this sorceress has made, but all in vain. My uncle hid the news and letters he got from St. Helena, saying that this silence ought to be enough to convince us. Mama is very devout and gives a lot of money to this woman; she is in league with her confessor, who in his turn is the right-hand man of yet other priests! It's all a horrible plot, and Colonna abets it. He's in church from morning to evening.'

And a few days later, to the same correspondent: 'The result is that all the letters Madame and the Cardinal have received for the last two years are treated as false: false signature, letters made up by the English government to make people believe the Emperor is still at St. Helena, whereas the Cardinal and Madame say they have positive proof that His Majesty has been carried off by angels and transported into a country where his health is excellent, and that they get news from him.'*

The Cardinal's letters are also full of the same crazy illusion. 'I do not know by what means God will free the Emperor from captivity,' he wrote to Las Cases, 'but I am none the less convinced that it will be soon. I expect everything from Him and my trust is complete.' And again: 'You must have gathered from all our letters how certain we are of the deliverance and the time it occurred, although the gazettes and the English still try to insinuate that he is at St. Helena, we have every reason to believe

* Planat de la Faye: *Rome et Sainte-Hélène de 1815 à 1821* (1862).

that he is not, and despite the fact that we do not know where he is or when he will give signs of life, we have enough proofs to make us persist in our beliefs and even hope that in a short while we shall learn the truth in a humanly certain manner. There can be no doubt that the gaoler of St. Helena is making Comte Bertrand write to you as if Napoleon were still in his clutches.'

For him, as for his sister, any quack doctor would do, as the Emperor was no longer on the rock: 'The little caravan left Rome just when we ourselves felt sure that they wouldn't get to St. Helena because there was someone who assured us that three or four days before January 19 the Emperor was given permission to leave St. Helena, and that in fact the English took him elsewhere. What can I say? Everything is miraculous in his life, and I'm much inclined to believe in yet one more miracle.'

As for Madame Mère she was delighted by the intervention of the angels, and consequently reassured as to Nabulio's fate, also his letters of the last part of 1819 and of 1820 hardly alluded to St. Helena. It was clear that she would eventually sail to the United States to see Joseph. Her health was satisfactory. The Cardinal was well ... She was rather worried about Pauline, and also Jerome who was suffering from 'gastric fever'. She would take the waters at Albano, where she had a villa bought from Louis. He was at Florence. She was smoothing out a quarrel between the Cardinal and the ex-King of Holland, which took a nasty turn when the nephew wrote to his uncle: 'Not a day passes without Your Eminence insulting me somehow or other ... You respond to decent behaviour with nothing but abuse, and a tone one can only find among Swiss and porters ... From this moment I shall forget I have an uncle called Fesch.' Louis always had a bad character ... Madame was in despair ... But it was no way to treat a Cardinal and remind him of his Swiss origins.

In August 1820, troubles began in earnest. Elisa, the former little scholar of Madame de Maintenon's school, and ex-Grand Duchess of Tuscany, who was living in gilded exile at Trieste, suddenly died at the age of forty-three 'of a putrid and bilious fever'. In July 1821, the Abbé Buonavita returned from St. Helena and called at the Rinuccini Palace bringing alarming news of the Emperor's health and a letter for Princess Pauline.

'He has had a succession of relapses since the middle of last year and every day deterioration is obvious. He is extremely weak... His liver ailment is now accompanied by another disease endemic in the island... The Emperor cannot eat meat, bread or vegetables, he keeps alive on clear soups and jellies.' Madame Mère was incredulous; she sent a message to the Cardinal, who came running, followed by Pauline. 'Mama and my uncle still don't really believe that the Abbé Buonavita left the Emperor at St. Helena; they said to me: "I don't believe any of it, the Emperor isn't there any more. I know it,"' wrote Napoleon's sister. 'I threw myself at Mama's feet... After a terrible scene between us, Mama's beliefs began to be shaken, but it was such a violent scene that I have quarrelled with the Cardinal and never want to see him again... It's very lucky that the Abbé had a letter to give to me in person; otherwise everything would have been kept from me.'

It was Pauline too, Nabulio's favourite sister, who wrote at once to the British Prime Minister: 'I beg to be allowed to go to St. Helena, to join the Emperor and receive his last breath... I know that Napoleon's hours are numbered, and I shall reproach myself for the rest of my life if I do not use every means in my power to sweeten his last moments and give him proof of my devotion.' Madame Mère still hesitated to believe, and yet... On May 5, in the evening, at the exact hour when the Emperor was dying six thousand kilometres away, a mysterious stranger called at the Rinuccini Palace and asked to be received, saying that he brought information of the highest importance. After questioning him, they led him into Madame Mère's salon, where she was sitting with her chamberlain and her lady-in-waiting... The unknown man explained that he hoped for an audience with Madame Mère alone, whereupon Colonna and Rosa Mellini withdrew 'into an adjoining room, ready to return at the slightest summons'. The disturbing individual then declared:

'At this very moment Napoleon is free from his sufferings and is happy.'

He had taken a crucifix from under his clothes, and now terrified Madame Mère by saying:

'Highness, kiss the Redeemer and Saviour of your well-beloved son; after many long years you will again see this son who now causes you such deep sorrow, this son whose name once resounded in cities and hamlets alike ... Before that memorable day there will be many changes of government in France, there will be civil wars, much blood will be spilt, all Europe will be ablaze. But Napoleon the Great will return to speak to France, and all the countries of Europe will feel his influence. Such is the great work that Napoleon the Great is destined by the King of Kings to carry out.'

The stranger bowed and retired rapidly. Had this alarming scene, described in her diary by Madame de Sartrouville, one of Madame's ladies who heard it herself from the chamberlain, been carried out by an intermediary of the Austrian clairvoyante's to strengthen her influence on the old lady, or was it a mysterious phenomenon of premonition or telepathy? No one will ever know.

Pauline's tears and the tragic account given by the Abbé Buonavita at last opened her eyes, and on July 14, Madame Mère launched herself into the attack. Lucien was the first to be told: 'The Abbé Buonavita has just arrived in Rome. I think of appealing to the British Parliament. Give me your advice.' She enclosed a copy of her message to Lord Liverpool: 'The report sent me by the surgeon on the condition of my son, Napoleon, is confirmed by eye-witnesses and destroys my last hope of seeing my son again if he continues to be detained on St. Helena, and I am therefore addressing my prayers to you that he may return and be transferred to a European climate. A desolate mother's heart should be eloquent enough, but I prefer to rely on your humanity and your good feelings to supply the words.' Next she wrote in the same vein to Lord Holland, begging him to raise the question in Parliament: 'He who keeps count of all good actions, will know how to reward you.' She even wrote to Marie-Louise, the faithless wife, though she had not seen or communicated with her since their parting at Blois in April 1814.

'Madame,
'You have heard as I have of Napoleon's sufferings, and I have never doubted that this has caused you the sorrow that all your sentiments must have aroused in you. Nor do I doubt that those same sentiments have inspired you to take an interest in his unhappy fate, and that you have said and done all you can to rescue him from the captivity where his good faith and his loyalty have thrown him ... In spite of my uncertainty as to whether this letter will reach you, I owe it to myself and to you to let you know of your husband's state of health. Try all the means in your power. In spite of politics, you have the right to be heard, and powerful sovereigns have many ways of keeping him in Europe, not in a murderous climate such as St. Helena's, somewhere where he can take the waters and re-establish his shattered health. The chaplain who has just returned left him on March 17 last, stretched on a sofa, talking of you and his son, and in spite of his greatness of character, saying that if he is not soon got away from there we shall hear that his days are ended. Your Majesty will understand from the enclosures the true state of his health.
'I pray God that you keep well, and if you still think of me sometimes – of Napoleon's mother – be assured of my affection.'

It was late, too late in fact! Two days later the news of the Emperor's death reached Rome, but the Cardinal waited a week before informing his sister. Madame Mère shut herself up for nearly three weeks, not even answering the letters of sympathy from her family; she wouldn't see Fesch, but spent her time weeping and praying beside the marble bust, seeing perhaps beneath the aquiline mask, which sculptors always gave to her son's face, the sharp features of her child, Nabulio.

'My life ended with my son's,' she wrote in her *Souvenirs*. 'From that moment I renounced everything. No more visits in any society; no more theatres – my sole distraction in moments of melancholy. My children and nephews have continued to beg me to go to the theatre; I always refuse and regard their suggestion as an insult.'

She had worn mourning, a robe and turban of black merino, ever since Elisa's death. She would never leave it off again. On August 15, Nabulio's birthday, she wrote to the British Foreign Secretary, Lord Castlereagh:

'Milord,
'The mother of the Emperor Napoleon comes to plead that his enemies will return her son's ashes . . . Hurled from the summit of human greatness to the lowest degree of misfortune, I shall not try and soften the British Minister's heart by painting the sufferings of his noble victim . . . Even in remotest times, among the most barbarous races, hatred was not prolonged beyond the tomb . . . I claim my son's remains; no one has more right to them than a mother . . . My son no longer has need of honours; his name is glory enough . . . In the name of justice and humanity, I implore you not to refuse my prayer. I could appeal to the government, I would entreat His Britannic Majesty to obtain my son's remains; I gave Napoleon to France and to the world. In the name of God, in the name of all mothers, I come before you as a suppliant, my Lord, asking that my son's remains should not be refused me.'

The noble Lord did not reply, and a month later the British Embassy in Paris informed the executors of the Emperor's Will that as the British Government regarded itself as the trustees of the ashes of Napoleon Bonaparte it would return them to France as soon as the Cabinet of His Christian Majesty expressed the desire.

The executors of the Will, Generals Bertrand and Montholon and Louis Marchand, a handful of the last of the faithful, do not seem to have travelled to Rome, and for some time Madame Mère remained in ignorance of the circumstances of her son's death, and

'The Mother of all Sorrows'

his last wishes regarding her, which produced tears of tenderness and pride.

'I thank my good and very excellent mother, the Cardinal, my brothers Joseph, Lucien and Jerome, Pauline, Caroline, Julie, Hortense, Catherine, Eugène for all their interest in me.

'I bequeathe to Madame the silver night-light ...

'I bequeathe to Madame, my very kind and beloved mother, the busts, frames and small tables in my rooms and the sixteen silver eagles, which she will distribute amongst my brothers, sisters and nephews. I charge Coursot to take these things to her in Rome, as well as the Chinese chains and necklaces which Marchand is to take for Pauline.'

Professor Antommarchi was the only one who came to give her an account of Napoleon's death agony in the hope – which was not fulfilled – of cashing in on a 'devotion' which may well be suspected of having hastened the invalid's death, and Coursot the steward brought her the busts, frames and small tables from the mortuary chamber, among them a marble head of the King of Rome, on which the dying man fixed his eyes, and a bedside table.

'He left me these things,' the lady in black told her visitors ... 'My poor child! ... A little table and a bust, Oh it's not very gay to visit the Emperor's mother!'*

Pius VII had been very much moved to hear, from the lips of the Abbé Buonavita himself, that the Emperor had died 'in sentiments of veneration for the Catholic Church', but the Secretary of State, Cardinal Consalvi, and Louis XVIII's ambassador took care that the religious ceremonies ordered by Madame Mère in memory of her son should not include solemn services in the chief churches of the city. On July 30 the French Ambassador sent a report to his Court: 'Today masses are to start being celebrated for the repose of Bonaparte's soul in the church of Santa Maria di Loreto, near Trajan's piazza. These masses are ordered by the family. They always split up in the same way; Louis visits Madame Bonaparte often and she receives no one but him;

* *Le Magasin des Familles*, popular magazine.

Cardinal Fesch and her two grandchildren, Madame la Princesse Gabrielli and Madame la Comtesse de Possé (Lucien's daughters). Madame Bonaparte's health is very delicate. She always seems to show intense sorrow at the death of her son.'

Napoleon's death had relaxed that surveillance which allowed a diplomat to know what was happening even inside the Rinuccini Palace, and Madame Mère could at last enjoy having her children about her, and realise her wish to 'pass her days with as little sadness as possible' in their company. She had succeeded in dissuading Jerome from going to the United States, and instead he installed himself with his family in the imposing Torlonia Palace, bought from Lucien, and was given the title of Prince of Montfort by his father-in-law. Louis was in the Salviati Palace, and his elder son Napoleon-Louis was married to a daughter of Joseph's and lived in the Villa Paolina. Lucien was in his estates at Canino, but often visited Rome.

Jerome had grown no more settled in his habits; he lived in royal state, but would often look in at the Rinuccini Palace between two receptions, and gaily disturb the atmosphere of peace and contemplation surrounding his mother. He talked about the past and his money troubles, but Madame only listened with half an ear – for, really, if she were to listen to everything he and Lucien said . . . 'If necessary,' she wrote to the former, 'reduce your household, or even send them all away; it would be more honourable to fight misfortune and conquer it.' And to the latter, who offered to sell her his Roman palace: 'I should have been delighted to do what you ask if it had been in my power, but it's absolutely impossible. You know I've given away everything I could to everyone; now, I must think of myself.' And her advice to the whole family was:

'One must live according to one's position; if one isn't a king any more, it's ridiculous to pretend to be; it's enough to be an honest man. Rings ornament fingers, but they fall off and the fingers are still there.'*

* Baron Larrey: *Madame Mère*.

'The Mother of all Sorrows'

Exiled, impoverished and under surveillance though she was, she stuck to her principles. In 1823, when the King of the Two Sicilies made an official visit to Rome, the Cardinal Secretary of State gave orders for the Eternal City to be illuminated: his messenger called at the Rinuccini Palace, and Madame Mère made him an edifying speech in icy tones:

'Tell the Cardinal Minister from me that if the personage for whom this fête is held had caused the death of his nearest and dearest relation, he wouldn't light a candle in his honour.'

It was giving too much importance to the poor King of the Two Sicilies, 'a good worthy buffoon who eats with his fingers' as his wife called him, to risk a quarrel on his account with the all-powerful Cardinal Secretary of State, but Madame did not dislike a chance of showing that the passing years had not bowed her, nor diminished her pugnacity, nor cut into the rock from which she was carved.

VIII

'Open, eternal gates'

'You see my mother weeping over my brother's misfortunes,' Pauline said to the Duchesse d'Abrantès after Napoleon's death. 'Well, her grief won't kill her; she'll suffer a long time and her own unhappiness will be more dreadful than the Emperor's.'

It so happened that deaths in the family followed each other at an implacable rhythm, and from 1820 onwards Madame Mère's life reminds one of those paths across the Roman campagna bordered with tombs and invaded by wild flowers, that she loved so much.

In 1822 she seems to have been very ill, for in October of that year she wrote to one of her daughters-in-law: 'Here I am fully convalescent after the mortal illness from which Divine Providence thought fit to relieve me.' She was left with painful palpitations of the heart. Apart from one or two colds, this seventy-year-old had no other physical troubles. The rest of the family resisted the passage of time less well: Eugène de Beauharnais, who had become Duc de Leuchtenberg, died in 1824, and Pauline in 1825 – Pauline whose beautiful body Canova immortalised as Venus. After an agony lasting eighty days, the frivolous creature, 'Notre-Dame des Colifichets',* was laid to rest in the Borghese chapel, dressed (by some ultimate coquetry) in a splendid silk robe. 'We have lost our poor Pauline,' wrote Madame; 'you can

* 'Our Lady of the Trinkets'.

easily imagine our grief.* Next it was Lucien's third son, Paul-Marie, who was mortally wounded in 1826, when taking part in an expedition under Lord Cochrane in favour of Greek independence. Then in 1827 Jeanne, Lucien's daughter, wife of Prince Honorati, was carried off by a 'chest ailment' after having gone out into the cold night in her ball dress.

'They all die far away from me,' groaned their ancestress, 'and I sit all alone, weeping for them! Am I doomed to bury them all, after bringing them into the world?'

When old Saveria who had nursed Nabulio, disappeared in her turn in 1829, Madame admitted: 'She's a real loss.' The sole survivor from the distant past, she could sigh with Goethe: 'I seem to be a myth, even to myself.'

Her only happy moments had been the weddings of grandchildren: Charles-Lucien, Lucien's son, with Zenaïde, Joseph's daughter in 1822; and that of Napoleon-Louis, elder son of Louis with Charlotte, Joseph's other daughter in 1826. Napoleon-Louis was a very promising young man, proud of his name and dreaming of writing his uncle's history. Nothing could have pleased Madame Mère more and she gave him a lot of advice. 'Any details I could give you about the Emperor are too childish to go in his history; he showed the way to write it himself in his *Mémoires*. You must treat him as a public figure. It's the prodigies of his politics, his administration, and laws that must be passed on to posterity. It's the most difficult but the finest task of a historian. The Emperor must appear to posterity in all his colossal proportions. His life is so full that it would make several folio volumes if one was to enter into every detail; that would tire the reader and lessen the hero's stature.'

This history, so full of glory for France, was often to be

---

* After having dictated her Will on the morning she died, Pauline received the sacraments. Someone expressed astonishment to her confessor, Monseigneur Strabi, Bishop of Macerata, that she had received absolution so quickly, after a somewhat eventful existence. 'I knew what I was doing,' replied the holy man, 'and I would do it again if I had the chance.'

remembered in Paris ... As for the noise made by the collapse of the Bourbon's throne, it resounded as far as Rome and awakened the hopes of the Bonapartes.

*   *   *

In April 1830 Madame Mère was walking in the gardens of the Villa Borghese, that Roman marvel where man's ingenuity has rivalled the beauty of the site by clothing the ruins with evergreen oaks, and marrying the gurgling water to the rustling of the wind, when, entering a narrow path, she let go of her chamberlain's arm, missed her footing, fell and couldn't get up. Her doctors diagnosed a fracture of the neck of the femur, an often fatal accident for a woman of eighty. Cardinal Fesch gave her the last sacraments in the Pope's name, while the whole family – Louis, Jerome, Julie and her daughters, Lucien's wife and Caroline gathered round her bed. They waited ... they prayed ... and the old lady got better. Certainly she never walked again, as they were unable to set the fracture; she had to lie stretched on a sofa at first, and later to sit up, with her broken limb resting on a cushion, but she escaped from the usual complications following this dangerous accident.

Soon afterwards, a young journalist called Joseph Méry was received by her: he came into the temple of memory on tiptoe and with a beating heart. 'What first struck me was the silence reigning in such a sumptuous dwelling. The stairs were deserted; I crossed empty rooms and corridors. M.B. opened a door into a magnificent drawing-room and announced my name. A woman was half-lying on a chaise-longue: it was the Emperor's mother ... The drawing-room was decorated with fine pictures representing Napoleon's family. Nothing could have been more touching than this famous mother, with her children gone and their portraits surrounding her. Motionless on her chair, she seemed to me in pain, from physical causes, from her age and her memories, but heroically resigned. Her dress fitted her closely and revealed that she was extraordinarily thin, her hands were fleshless, nothing remained of her face but a pale epidermis, her wide-open eyes moved at random but didn't seem to have lost their sight ... From where I sat I could see both the motionless head of Napoleon's mother and the high tower of the Capitol. What a combination of names! The grandeur of Rome warring with the grandeur of a woman ... More virile than her son on the rock of St. Helena, she was clinging to the Tarpeian rock; despair hadn't made her throw herself from it: she wanted to live a long time, her forehead wearing her crown of unhappiness; she had long wished to fight against the massive ruins on the other side of the hill.'

In July Paris was in the hands of the Revolution chasing away the last of the Bourbons, Charles X. A few shouts of 'Long live Napoleon II' were heard, but it was the Duc d'Orléans who seized the throne and became King of the French ... A good politician, Madame Mère wrote to Queen Julie: 'The events now passing in France are not nearly over. A small faction has made use of a truly national movement and turned it to its advantage. God alone knows what will come of it all.' And a few days later, after the proclamation of the new king by a docile assembly, she added: 'Two hundred and nineteen deputies have decided the fate of the Nation without a mandate. I do not see how long France will be satisfied by such cavalier treatment.' There was in fact no plebiscite for this king who called himself a liberal, as there had been for Napoleon's Constitution of the year XII, though people are ready to call him a dictator.'*

One of her grandsons, Louis-Napoleon – the future Napoleon III, and a young man who seemed to walk 'preceded by his shadow' according to the expression of one of his contemporaries – was intensely interested in these events, burning with desire to rush to Paris and rally the supporters of his cousin, Napoleon II; but Madame Mère extinguished this fiery zeal with great good

* If is often useful to remember that the Constitution of the year XII, which established the Empire in France, was submitted to a referendum which produced 3.572.329 '*Oui*' for 2.579 '*Non*'.

sense: 'We must see whether the French people, who have so energetically and courageously thrown off the yoke imposed on them by the foreigner, will be fools enough to submit to a faction which has impudently and imprudently dared to solve a problem which concerns the whole Nation. In proclaiming the Duc d'Orléans king, before having obtained the Nation's assent, the Chamber of Deputies has broken all the principles of the Revolution and taken a terrible responsibility upon itself. You write like a young hothead. To judge the situation correctly, one must look at it coolly, and although I do not underestimate the vigour and courage of the Parisians, I am far from seeing a philosopher's revolution in these battles bravely fought by a few Frenchmen... Wait for events before judging them. You see I'm preaching. I hope you won't take offence: it is only that an old head, cooled by experience and time, is trying to instil reason into a young and ardent head that is dear to her. At your age it's better to have too much fire than too little.'*

But she needed great spirit, in that summer of 1830, to be interested in the events of a world she would soon have left, for the heat added to her sufferings, and each of her letters echoes her torments. 'They have tried more than once to get me to walk, but without success. It gives me great pain and I can't put my foot to the ground... Yesterday I sat up for more than an hour but it tired me very much; when I'm lying down I feel shooting pains in my leg and thigh at intervals, which are a severe trial... All I can do is sit up in my wheel chair for one or two hours.' Another source of misery, and one of the worst: afflicted by a double cataract, which the doctors refused to operate on because of the patient's age, Madame Mère progressively and rapidly lost her sight, and added blindness to infirmity; she could only spin and knit by touch.

There was no weakening of her faculties, however, nor of her will: she still steered the ship of the imperial family with a firm hand. Louis-Philippe's government, wishing to be liberal at all

---

* Rome, August 17, 1830.

costs and hoping to rally the numerous Bonapartists to their side, suddenly decided to carry out the clauses of the Treaty of Fontainebleau of 1814 guaranteeing pensions to the Emperor's relations, but still supported the law of exile. Madame Mère immediately lectured her family on the disadvantages of an offer she knew they were inclined to accept, and which had only to be 'solicited'. 'By such an act,' she wrote to Joseph's wife Julie, 'I should be doing all I could to annul what happened in 1815. It would be an outrage to the Emperor's memory, and we should be showing ourselves to be his son's worst enemies. Besides, there's something remarkably base in soliciting something from a government that has upheld the law of January 12, 1816, which banished us for ever. I'm sure you will reject the proposal with scorn ... Honour must always come before money ... We must be careful with what remains to us, and if we can't live royally, let us live as honourable individuals, and don't let us expose ourselves to humiliation, nor to the reproaches of our conscience.'

These events in Paris were the last things to give her pleasure: the men who had shared Napoleon's exile at St. Helena were honoured and given important posts, marshals of the Empire were summoned to support the throne, a deputy proposed to recommend the return of the Emperor's remains to Paris, and Madame Mère smiled as Chateaubriand's remark was read to her: 'Why forbid the relations of the man who dominated Europe to enter France, and yet open the door to his ashes? The latter are much more dangerous ... They will become active at every anniversary of their victories; every day, from under their column, they will say to each quasi-legitimist passer-by: What have you done with our national honour?'*

At the end of 1831 a decree was passed ordering that the statue of the Emperor should be replaced on top of the column by one made from the melted bronze of 1,200 cannons taken at

---

* The project foresaw that Napoleon's remains would be placed under the Vendôme Column. Chateaubriand never forgave Louis-Philippe for 'selling off' the national honour by consenting to do anything to keep the peace.

'Open, eternal gates!'

Austerlitz. Jerome brought his mother the great news. She was dozing. The ex-King of Westphalia leaned over her.

'Mother, can you hear me?'

She looked up in surprise.

'Well, mother, I've just had news from France. The Emperor's statue is to be replaced on the Column!'

The old lady grew agitated, and raised her thin hands to heaven, moaning and sobbing with joy.

'... Heavens ... the Emperor's statue! Heavens ... the Emperor's statue on the column!'*

There was also to be an issue by the French Mint of one hundred and sixty-five medals commemorating the great events of the Consulate and Empire, and an incredible number of plays soon appeared dealing with the Man of the Legend, whose names Madame Mère listened to with joy day after day: *Bonaparte, lieutenant of Artillery, Napoleon at Berlin or the grey overcoat, Napoleon at Schoenbrunn and St. Helena, Napoleon at Brienne, Malmaison and St. Helena, The Grenadier of Wagram.* She knew that the actor Gobert was applauded because he bore such a strange resemblance to Nabulio, and that the unfortunate who played the part of Hudson Lowe couldn't get home without police protection. She knew that there was also a vaudeville called *Napoleon in Paradise* whose last lines, recited by a soldier of the Old Guard to an astonished St. Peter were:

> '*Vous craignez qu'un jour de goguette*
> *Le Caporal dise au Bon Dieu*
> *Ote-toi de là que je m'y mette.*'

But her favourite piece was Alexandre Dumas' *Napoleon Bonaparte*, with five acts and twenty-four tableaux, all 'written in eight days' and including eighty characters. What a change from the silence imposed by the Bourbons' censure from 1815 to 1830! History is indeed the conscience of nations.

* * *

* Jerome Bonaparte: *Mémoires.*

'Open, eternal gates!'

In November 1830 Queen Hortense came to live at Rome to the great joy of Madame Mère, who didn't forget that it was at Malmaison with the ex-Queen of Holland that Napoleon sought refuge after his abdication, and that Josephine's daughter had compromised herself in the eyes of the Allies by her filial behaviour. Pope Pius VII had just died and the Romans were much taken up with preparations for the Conclave which was to elect Gregory VII, in other words in a great state of excitement, highly satisfying to the Queen's two sons, Napoleon-Louis and Louis-Napoleon, who were dreaming of plots and risings to liberate Italy from Austrian domination, and perhaps to restore their cousin, Duke of Reichstadt and King of Rome, to power... One of Queen Hortense's ladies-in-waiting, and Josephine's godchild, was Valérie Mazuyer. She was an admiring visitor, already trembling on the eve of her first audience: 'I feel I shall die of fear when I see this old lady who held Napoleon in her arms as a baby, who saw him feeble and small, who brought this colossal power into the world and still survives.' Next day: 'Madame Mère lives in the Rinuccini Palace at the corner of the Corso and the Piazza di Venezia. As she now never leaves her rooms her face is as pale as a ghost, so that she looks like one of the busts surrounding her. All these marble heads keep her company, although she guesses at their presence by memory rather than sees them: in fact she is going blind, and reading or handwork are out of the question for her... This woman's intelligence has kept all its liveliness. One can't ask her advice without finding in her the same reasoning power, the same clear judgement that we admired in the Emperor. The misfortune of the Bonapartes, she says, is to be scattered and so divided. She reasons about it all with extraordinary force and exactness.'

Infected by the revolutionary fever devouring all Italy, and led away by her impetuous grandsons, did Madame Mère sometimes abandon her self-imposed reserve? Some say she did, there are documents supporting the view... Queen Hortense's two sons rode round Rome waving a tricolour flag, at a critical moment when the republican revolution had extended throughout the peninsula and removed a number of 'tyrants', including the ex-Empress Marie-Louise, from their thrones. Afterwards they flung themselves openly into the fray, taking part in a plot aimed at arresting groups of cardinals at the time of the Conclave, and proclaiming Napoleon II king of the Italian confederation. This coup was planned for December 10, 1830, and Madame Mère seems to have promised a hundred crowns to anyone who set up the tricolour flag, symbol of liberty, in the Eternal City, and a million francs to the Minister of Finance of the future Roman government who rallied to the cause of the Emperor's son. The affair turned out badly, the accomplices possibly having been police *agents provocateurs*. There were some killed and the Queen's sons fled in haste.

'Your children should think of leaving Italy without delay,' advised the grandmother to the mother of the two hotheads. 'I tremble at the thought of seeing them fall into Austrian hands, and that will infallibly happen if they delay too long.' If she had no fears for herself it was because Cardinal Fesch had intervened in her favour with the new Pope, who had frequented the Rinuccini Palace when he was still merely *Papabile*, but Jerome must leave Rome at once and take refuge at Florence. A hope disappointed, and one of the Queen's sons – Napoleon-Louis– the husband of Charlotte – died during the flight.* 'The severe blow that has just struck us was all the more terrible because unexpected. Time alone can heal such a cruel wound.' But there was worse to come. Another Bonaparte, Elisa's daughter the Countess Camerata went to Vienna to sound Napoleon's son; being under close surveillance he sent his friend Prokesch von

* Napoleon-Louis' death was officially the result of measles, but shortly afterwards sinister rumours were being circulated. Well-informed witnesses, such as Baron Larrey, former surgeon to Napoleon's Imperial Guard, and Valérie Mazuyer, lady-in-waiting to Queen Hortense, stated that the Prince had received a dagger-wound, on orders from the Carbonari, and that the measles finished off a dying man. The truth was concealed to spare his mother and grandmother.

Osten, his confidant and a young officer who exercised a strange influence over him, to see her, but the interview had been disappointing. 'She was very reserved with me,' Prokesch wrote in his *Journal*, 'and didn't trust me at all; nor did I her. I told her that her imprudence was sure to have been noticed by the police; that as a result she might cause the duke useless embarrassment and of course have an adverse effect on such liberty as he is allowed. I spoke to her warmly about his person and character, and told her he was absolutely free to occupy himself with his father's history, and that he had a passion for studying it... She listened to all this with visible astonishment and pleasure. I expressed some doubts about the strength of the party that was ready to support the Emperor's son. She had nothing to tell me on the subject, except generalities which indicated her hopes, but not her proposed actions.'

How mortifying his grandmother must have found the attitude of this grandson of hers, of this young man who hesitated to take a decision or embark on an adventure! He was surrounded by policemen, spies and false friends, it is true, but if only he had shown some of Nabulio's temperament!

It fell to the blind, helpless octogenarian, mourning some of the dearest of her family and exiled by those who had acclaimed her for so long, to be the mainstay of the others during those bad days – Julie, whose husband seemed in no hurry to return to Europe; Lucien, fighting his creditors; Jerome, bored to death at Florence; and above all poor little Charlotte, Napoleon-Louis' widow at twenty-eight. And how firmly she wrote at regular intervals: 'My dear child, I urge you to try and overcome your sorrow, for to forget altogether must be impossible for you ... Comfort your mother; her state of health grieves me ... Remember, my dear Charlotte, that God sends us good as well as bad, and that we must be resigned and bless the hand that strikes us ... I enjoin you to be strong and brave; remember that this life is only a vale of sorrow and tears and that every day teaches us to withdraw from it ... How many disappointed hopes! ... Misfortune is one of the duties of existence, to be accepted firmly, however bitter.' Bowed by years and illness, feeling her loneliness more cruelly now that she saw the Cardinal less often, what strength of spirit she showed, and each of her letters reflected her battle against adversity: 'For nearly a month the pain I have suffered every day often prevents my sleeping ... I only get up for a few hours, and that is to rest on my sofa, only two feet from my bed ... I am very isolated now, all my children are far away.' Her letters to Joseph, Jerome, Queen Hortense or Queen Julie were now signed by Rosa Mellini or Madame de Sartrouville, her lady-in-waiting, for her hand was too weak to hold the pen and her eyes were plunged in endless night. Her fixed pupils and marble face gave her a terrifying majesty which left her visitors speechless. One of these was the mysterious Prokesch von Osten, who left the Duke of Reichstadt dying at Vienna, and presented himself one day at the Rinuccini Palace, where his grandmother was herself preparing to descend into the tomb.

No, there was no question of a plot. How could agitation be fomented between the little prince (about whom the Austrian chancellor wrote to his ambassadors: 'The Duke's illness is a typical case of pulmonary phthisis, and if this is a ruthless disease at any age it is fatal at twenty-one') and the blind mother of dead and exiled sovereigns. Charged with a mission to the Holy See by Metternich towards the middle of February 1832, Prokesch had simply promised Napoleon's son that he would 'see' the Bonapartes – nothing more ... Such at least is the officially accepted version, but one would like to think that the son, carried away by events in France and the great public enthusiasm of July 1830 and dominated by the thought of his father's genius, had dreamt of trying his luck and had won over the highly secretive Prokesch – who, moreover, noted in his *Journal* on November 29, 1930, at the time of his interview with the Countess Camerata: 'The duke asked me to give him my word of honour that he could count on me in even the most serious circumstances.' Prokesch got to know Prince Gabrielli and his wife Charlotte Bonaparte, daughter of

'Open, eternal gates!'

Lucien's first marriage; he spoke to them about his intimacy with the duke, the young exile's hopes, and his ambition to reign over France some day. This conversation, repeated to Madame Mère, must have served Prokesch as an introduction and smoothed over any obstacles raised by his being an Austrian diplomat. On July 21 Princess Gabrielli took him to the Rinuccini Palace and presented him to her grandmother. 'The emotion she showed and the tears she shed moved me profoundly,' wrote the young Austrian. 'She spoke like a dying and broken-hearted woman about the danger threatening the Prince's life. As I was still full of hope, I succeeded in calming her and distracting her by the interest she took in what I had to tell.* She gradually got command of herself, and made me talk about the Prince's tastes, qualities and way of life; she questioned and listened tirelessly.'

What joy to hear that this child, brought up as an archduke, venerated his father's memory and wished to get to know his paternal family, as well as that he was intelligent and gifted with numerous talents.

'While the Prince is full of ability to get to the bottom of things, he is slow to grasp them at first,' admitted Prokesch.

'He's like his father in that,' interrupted Madame Mère; 'when Napoleon first started school I was less hopeful for him than for any of my children. It was a long time before he made progress; one day, when he got a good report he hurried to bring it to me full of delight, and after he'd shown it me he put it on a chair and sat on it with the expression of a conqueror.'

She also spoke about the day in 1814 when she had embraced the pretty fair child for the last time. During eighteen years she had had no news of him! Was it possible to be so cruel to an old woman? The Empress herself had never answered her letters. Had she received them? And the Austrian ambassador at Rome had never called on her! Tears rolled down her impassive face.

* The final phase of the disease which was to carry off Napoleon's son had begun after Prokesch left Vienna.

'Tell my grandson always to respect his father's last wishes. His hour will come. He will sit on the throne of France.'*

'I kissed her hand and prepared to take my leave,' went on Prokesch, 'but she held me back and seemed to be making a supreme effort to stand up. She seemed to grow in stature and an air of majestic dignity surrounded her. Then I felt that she was trembling; she laid her two hands on my head. I guessed what she wanted and knelt down.

'"As I cannot go to him," she said, "may the blessing of his grandmother, who will soon leave this world, be on your head. My prayers, my tears, my thoughts will be with him until the last instant of my life; take him what I have laid on your head, what I entrust to your heart."

'Princess Charlotte supported her. I stood up, she embraced him, and remained for a long while silently leaning on his shoulder. We led her to the sofa. I kissed her hand again and left her to Charlotte's care.'

During the evening Madame Mère's secretary brought him a box of games that had belonged to the Emperor and had been sent back from St. Helena, and a miniature of herself when young, with a lock of Napoleon's hair on the back, to be given to the Duke of Reichstadt. By a strange coincidence, on the following day, in the room at Schoenbrunn where Napoleon slept after Austerlitz and stretched on a camp-bed like his father's, the life of the former heir to the most powerful Empire of modern Europe was extinguished, and he breathed his last sad words in German:

'*Ich gehe unter . . . Ich gehe unter . . .*'

His death allowed Marie-Louise to make a final break with the past, but she wrote her mother-in-law the letter imposed by protocol.

---

* In his Will Napoleon wrote: 'I recommend my son never to forget that he was born a French prince, and never to lend himself to being made a tool in the hands of triumvirs who oppress the peoples of Europe. He must never fight against France, nor harm it in any way. He should adopt my motto: Everything for the French people.'

'Madame,

In the hope of softening the bitterness of the sad news that it is my unfortunate duty to announce to you, I would not yield to anyone else the painful task of communicating it.

On Sunday 22, at five o'clock in the morning, my beloved son the Duke of Reichstadt succumbed to his long and cruel sufferings. I had the consolation of being with him during his last moments, and also of being able to convince myself that nothing had been neglected which might have saved his life. But medical aid was impotent against a disease of the chest which from the first the doctors unanimously judged so dangerous that it must infallibly carry my unhappy son to the grave at an age when he aroused the fairest hopes. It was God's will! Nothing remains for us but to submit to His will, and to mingle our sorrow and our tears.

In these tragic circumstances, please accept, Madame, this expression of the attachment and consideration felt for you by your affectionate,
  Marie-Louise.'

The Rinuccini Palace went into mourning, but Madam Mère couldn't make up her mind to write to her forgetful daughter-in-law and it was the Cardinal who signed the following frigid letter:

'Madame,

In spite of the political stupidity which has always interfered with my receiving news of my beloved child whose loss you have announced, I have never ceased having the feelings of a mother towards him. He was still an object of some consolation to me, but at my great age it has been God's will to add to my other habitual and painful infirmities this further blow, and sign of His grace, in the firm hope of having amply compensated for the glory of this world with his own.

Please accept my gratitude, Madame, for taking the trouble in these grievous circumstances to try to ease the bitterness of my soul. Rest assured that it will persist throughout my remaining years.

Since my state of health prevents my signing this letter, permit me to entrust it to my brother.'

But Queen Hortense was the recipient to whom she poured out her sorrow in simple, Christian terms.

'My dear daughter,
I have been given your letter of August 17. It finds me very ill and overcome with grief. I am trying to take courage, but there are some sorrows one cannot brace oneself to bear. The blow that has just struck us is one of these. It has reopened all the barely healed wounds in my heart, and every day I learn new details to increase my grief. It breaks my heart to realise that in such short a space of time so many children whom I counted on to close my eyes have themselves been hurled into the tomb by premature death, just when they were full of promise.'

Obeying the wish expressed in the Emperor's Will, she had made the Duke of Reichstadt her sole legatee: everything she possessed came from Napoleon's generosity, and it was to have reverted to his son. Now that the heir to this great name was dead in the flower of his age, she rewrote her last wishes on September 22, 1832. They are an added proof of the sense of justice and order which she had transmitted to the greatest of her sons. In view of the state of her eyes, the deed was drawn up by a notary and read aloud to her in the presence of eight witnesses, who signed it. She declared that she died in the Catholic religion, repenting of her sins. The Cardinal was to be entrusted with having her body buried in the church she had chosen; ten thousand masses were to be said for the repose of her soul. Next she enumerated bequests to the clergy and the poor and provided for those who had served her – Colonna, Rosa Mellini, Bernard Touvenin and Edouard Dambré (her men-servants), Robaglia (her secretary) and Dr. Carlo Antonini (her doctor). She left the family portraits to the Cardinal; her four sons were residuary legatees 'of equal shares', Caroline and Elisa's children only receiving their legal shares. She left about three million francs, of which one million was entrusted to the Cardinal to be divided directly among the family. It was a considerable fortune, but if one remembers that she left France in 1815 with something in the neighbourhood of thirteen million, her generosity towards her family in bad times can be measured. She had taken care also to destroy all the notes making her children her debtors, except one from Caroline for 300,000 francs and it is not known who benefited most from her bounty.

Having thus put her own affairs in order she attacked the difficult task of collecting together Napoleon's various legacies to his son, deposited by him with his companions at St. Helena. It was not a question of money, for the Emperor disposed of his capital among his friends and servants at Longwood, but there were relics, and arms in particular, which Joseph was anxious to see given to the Nation. The bounties Napoleon bestowed on Europe will be talked of for many years to come and he listed them himself at St. Helena: they range from the docks at Antwerp to the maritime works of Venice, from roads, canals and bridges to 'causeways surpassing in audacity grandeur and art all that the Roman's made', from much beautiful architecture in Paris and Lyons to four hundred sugar-beet factories, from the Musée Napoleon to breeds of horse and merino sheep ... Only a few objects were saved from the disaster at St. Helena and found their way home, but what objects they were! There were his campaign beds, his uniforms, his linen, his books, his silver, relics left to his son 'in memory of a father whom the whole Universe will talk to him about'.

Madame Mère commissioned her cousin, General Arrighi de Casanova, Duke of Padua, a veteran of Marengo and Wagram, to act for her and on her instructions, but dealings with the trustees were long and bitter owing to their fear that now that the Duke of Reichstadt was dead the treasure would be scattered to the four corners of Europe. She had to intervene more than once, and sternly, to get satisfaction. 'Concerning the great inheritance left by the Emperor, Monsieur le Maréchal,' she wrote to General Bertrand, former Grand Marshal, 'I am called upon by law to dispose of it and I cannot yield either the property itself or use of it to anyone except by my own action and in circumstances chosen by me ... I hope there will be no desire to use violence and replace justice by force ... Owing to the confidence your experience gives me, I feel assured that you will find it convenient to get rid of such a great trust by handing it to its rightful owner, who is only interested to see that it contributes to the greater glory of the Emperor.'

Three years passed before the battle ended, and then by the end of 1835 the Duke of Padua was at last in possession of all the objects except the arms ... Did Paris get wind of Madame Mère's intention to restore the relics, was there pity for her great age and isolation? One of the deputies let it be known that he was to ask for an exception to the law of exile to be made in favour of the Emperor's mother. He showed little knowledge of the old lady!

'Monsieur,' she wrote to him, 'those persons who realise the absurdity of maintaining the law of exile for my family and who nevertheless suggest making an exception for me, can never have known my principles, nor my character.

'I became a widow at thirty-three and my eight children were my sole consolation. Corsica was threatened with separation from France: losing my possessions and abandoning my home had no terrors for me. I followed my children to the Continent: in 1814 I followed Napoleon to the isle of Elba, and in 1816 in spite of my age I would have followed him to St. Helena if he had not forbidden it. I therefore resigned myself to live in Rome, as a prisoner of the State. I do not know whether it was by an expanded interpretation of the law that I was exiled from France, or by protocol of the Allied powers. I then saw that persecution would eventually force those members of my family who might devote themselves to keeping me company by living in Rome, to leave that city, and I decided to renounce the pleasure of their presence and hope only for happiness in a future life ... What equivalent could I find in France, that would not be poisoned by the injustice of the men in power, who cannot forgive my family the glory it has won?

'Leave me alone therefore with my honourable sorrows, to carry the integrity of my character to the tomb. I will never separate my fate from that of my children: it is my only remaining consolation.'

She was unwilling to owe anything to the country and the people who had exiled her, but she held with strange tenacity to her plan of returning the most precious souvenirs of Napoleon to Paris, because her good sense told her that France would one day remember the greatest man in her history and set up a worthy monument to him. On January 26, 1836, at the age of eighty-six she was still rebuking the Duke of Padua: 'I am writing today to beg you immediately to elucidate everything to do with my estate, so that I can come to a decision and put everything in order as soon as possible, and dispose of it as I think fit.' She insisted 'as soon as possible.' ... She was in a hurry to end it all.

Next day she was feverish and complained of a chill. For four days she remained in that strange country between life and the unknown, in which the dying stray with eyes closed. Jerome and Lucien came to her bedside. On February 2, just before seven in the evening she seemed to be dozing: without a word, without a groan, like a lamp running out of oil, her life was extinguished...

Her embalmed body lay in state for two days in a drawing room watched over by four silver eagles. A scupltor took a cast of her face.* An artist drew the features whose fame was due only to their resemblance to her son's. Monks and nuns prayed around her, starting at the sound of the fireworks going up in the Corso, where a battle of flowers and confetti was in full swing: Carnival

* The Danish sculptor, B. Thorvaldsen, lived in Rome from 1821 to 1838. There are two casts in the Thorvaldsen Museum, Copenhagen; one is the death mask, but it is difficult to decide which.

was at its height and the youth of Rome were wearing masks and making a great uproar. On the 4th the funeral service took place in the church of Santa Maria in Via Lata. No pomp, by order of the Holy See. Stendhal even assures us that Gregory XVI's police hissed the coffin during its journey from the palace to the church – a strange concept of an apostolic mission ... No imperial arms hung on the church door. And what would have been the use? On the catafalque were the initials L.R.B., and beneath them a band bearing two words which said everything:

MATER NAPOLEONIS

The death certificate tells us that during the following night the body was taken to Corneto, the Tarquinies of antiquity, near Civita-Vecchia and buried in the convent of the Sisters of the Holy Cross and Passion. Her stay there was short, for between 1855 and 1858 Napoleon III had a mausoleum built at Ajaccio which was to be the sepulchre of the Bonaparte family, and Madame Mère's body was taken there in 1859, after having rested for some time in the Cathedral where she had been married as a radiantly beautiful young girl. On the black marble slab over the recess is an inscription that is not without nobility: 'Maria Letizia Ramolino-Bonaparte, Mater Regum.' On April 5, 1951 she was at last joined by the remains of Carlo Bonaparte, the husband she had loved so much and who had fathered an imposing line: an emperor, three kings, a prince, a princess and a grand-duchess.

Some people have wished to see Madame Mère lying beneath the gilt dome of the Invalides, close to Napoleon, Joseph, Jerome and the King of Rome. It would be a spectacular amends for the outrage inflicted by her banishment and exile in Rome, and the Emperor's mother deserved this unprecedented honour, but Madame Letizia was a simple-hearted woman, who descended from the pedestal she had been placed on to say laughingly to the surprised Court: 'No one in the world has spanked so many kings and queens as I have.' Her face would have clouded at the thought of becoming a historical monument.

'Open, eternal gates!'

It was at Ajaccio, in the rue Fesch smelling of *uziminu*, *broccio* and fried fish, two steps from the Casa Bonaparte and the Cathedral, and beside the husband she survived for fifty-one years, that she herself would have chosen to lie, in that same silence and dust.

* * *

Letizia Bonaparte was lifted out of obscurity by her son's dazzling rise to fame: if Nabulio had merely been a simple officer in the French army she would have remained a bourgeoise housewife, passing her uneventful days between a husband to whom she was perfectly obedient, according to Corsican law, and children who would have taken all her time. Transported to the front rank of public life by events she found more terrifying than dazzling, she became Madame Mère – that is to say a very great personage, but without ever falling into what Stendhal calls 'the miseries of vanity which exhaust all enthusiasm for princes and princesses'.

The facts that Napoleon added feelings of admiration and gratitude to the filial love he bore her like any other bourgeois son in the world, that he always considered 'his good and excellent mother' as the head of the family in preference to his elder brother Joseph, are evidence of Madame Letizia's upright, noble and forceful character: she never intrigued like the two queen-mothers of the Medici family who reigned over Charles IX, Henri III and Louis XIII in France, or like Maria-Feodorovna, the dowager-empress of Russia, who dominated the Tsar Alexander. Cut off by widowhood at an age when a woman is still charming and courted, she never once thought of an alliance of any sort – even a secret one, like her Habsburg-Lorraine daughter-in-law Marie-Louise, who was an adulteress at the age of twenty-five and contracted her third marriage at forty-three! 'Few lives have been so free from hypocrisy, and in my view so noble,' as even the discriminating Stendhal was pleased to say.

A fine character, greatness of spirit, religion, nobility and pride, she bequeathed all these to the son who spoke of her so often in the evening of his days, as he walked round and round his garden at Longwood like a prisoner. 'The Emperor remarked that at that exact moment he still remembered the lessons of pride he had received in childhood, and that they had influenced him all his life,' noted Las Cases. Madame Mère's was a strong spirit that had been tempered by colossal events; she had experienced five or six revolutions; her house was burned three times by Corsican factions. 'Give up your opposition,' Paoli had said to her; 'it will destroy you and yours, your fortune; the evil results will be incalculable and nothing will mend them.' Madame replied, like a heroine from Corneille, that she only knew two laws: she, her children and her family only recognised duty and honour.

The relationship between the Emperor and Madame Letizia has certainly led more than one contemporary astray: the omnipotent son has been accused of not showing his mother all the care and forethought she was entitled to, and the mother – always sparing of words – of not giving her son enough proofs of her affection. This is to show ignorance of the life of a typical Corsican family, to whom fulsomeness is antipathetic. Their love was stern and silent and one must look less to public embraces than to actions for signs of the bonds uniting these two strong and exceptional beings. From the moment Fortune smiled on him, General Bonaparte wanted to have his mother beside him and to help her to restore the family house; when Destiny was unkind, the frugal Madame Mère offered him her purse and her jewels, which she prized highly, to protect him against hard times.

Madame Mère must not merely be thought of as an austere old lady who amused the Court with her Corsican patois, nor as a housewife with rustic tastes and endowed with obstinate and careful frugality, she was honourable, inflexible, admirable in her constancy and faithful self-sacrifice, in a word she was worthy to be Napoleon's mother.

Select Bibliography

Abrantès (Duchesse d') – *Mémoires*
Antommarchi (Dr.) – *Les derniers moments de Napoléon*
Augustin-Thierry (A.) – *Madame Mère*
Barras (Vicomte de) – *Mémoires*
Bartel (Paul) – *La Jeunesse inédite de Napoléon*
Bartel (Paul) – *Napoléon à l'île d'Elbe*
Bausset (de) – *Mémoires*
Bertaut (Jules) – *Le roi Jérôme*
Beugnot (Comte) – *Mémoires*
Blessington (Countess of) – *The Idler in Italy*
Bonaparte (Jerome) – *Mémoires*
Bonaparte (Louis) – *Documents historiques et réflexions sur le Gouvernement de la Hollande*
Bonaparte (Lucien) – *Mémoires*
Bourienne (Louis-Antoine de) – *Mémoires*
Bradi (Lorenzo di) – *La vraie figure de Napoléon en Corse*
Campbell (Major-General Sir Neil) – *Napoleon at Fontainebleau and Elba, being a Journal of occurrences in 1814–15*
Chaptal (Jean-Antoine) – *Souvenirs sur Napoléon*
Charles-Roux (F.) – *Rome asile des Bonaparte*
Chateaubriand – *Mémoires d'Outre-Tombe*
Chuquet (A.) – *La jeunesse de Napoléon*
Ciana (Albert) – *Les Bonaparte*
Cochelet (Mlle.) – *Mémoires sur la reine Hortense et la famille impériale*
Constant – *Mémoires*
Decaux (A.) – *Letizia. Mère de l'Empereur*
Dupont (M.) – *Le tragique destin du duc d'Enghien*
Fouché (J., duc d'Otrante) – *Mémoires*
Gourgaud (général baron) – *Journal de Sainte-Hélène*

Bibliography

Gregori (J.) – *Nouvelle histoire de la Corse*
Hortense (Reine) – *Mémoires*
Jung (Th.) – *Lucien Bonaparte et ses Mémoires*
Labarre de Raillicourt (D.) – *Louis Bonaparte*
Larrey (Baron) – *Madame Mère*
Las Cases (Comte de) – *Mémorial de Sainte-Hélène*
Lévy (Arthur) – *Napoléon intime*
Lucas–Dubreton (J.) – *Le culte de Napoléon*
Madelin (Louis) – *Histoire du Consulat et de l'Empire*
Marchand (Louis) – *Mémoires*
Marco-Saint-Hilaire (E.) – *Mémoires d'un page*
Masson (Frédéric) – *Napoléon et sa famille*
Masuyer (Valérie) – *Mémoires*
Mathilde (Princesse) – *Souvenirs*
Mèneval (Baron) – *Souvenirs*
Misciattelli (Piero) – *Lettere de Letizia Buonaparte*
Montholon (Charles-Tristan de) – *Récits de la captivité*
Morgan (Lady) – *Passages from my autobiography*
Napoléon I – *Correspondance*
Napoléon (Prince, et J. Hanateau) – *Mémoires de la reine Hortense*
Nasica (T.) – *Mémoires sur l'enfance et la jeunesse de Napoléon I*
Peretti (L.) – *Letizia Bonaparte*
Peyre (R.) – *Napoléon I et son temps*
Pons de l'Hérault – *Souvenirs et anecdotes de l'île d'Elbe*
Prokesch von Osten (Graf) – *Mein Verhaltniss zum Herzog von Reichstadt*
Prokesch von Osten (Graf) – *Aus den Tagebüchern des Grafen Prokecsh von Osten*
Rémusat (Madame de) – *Mémoires*
Sartrouville (Madame de) – *Journal*
Talleyrand (Prince de) – *Mémoires*
Thiers (A.) – *Histoire du Consulat et de l'Empire*
Ussher (Captain Sir Thomas – A narrative of events connected with the first abdication of the Emperor Napoleon, his embarkation at Fréjus and voyage to Elba on board H.M.S. *Undaunted*. (Dublin, 1841)

Index

Abrantès, Duc d' (*see* Junot, General)
Abrantès, Duchesse d', 48n, 53n, 64n, 66, 68–71, 73, 82n, 85n
Aix, seminary of, 13, 23, 28
Aix-la-Chapelle, 92–3, 102–3, 106, 110
Ajaccio, 1–8, 10, 13, 15–17, 20–1, 23, 25, 27–30, 40, 68, 117, 126–7, 186–7; Madame Mère revisits, 43–6
Alexander I, Tsar of Russia, 81, 88, 90, 109, 113, 118, 120, 158, 187
Antibes, Napoleon at, 33–4
Antommarchi, Dr., 18, 165
Antonini, Dr. Carlo, 182
Antwerp, 183
Ariosto, 69
Arnault, 42
Artois, Charles, Comte d' (*see* Charles X)
Aurel, bookseller, 20
Austerlitz, battle of, 74, 173–4
Autun, 13–14
Avignon, Napoleon at, 32

Bacchiochi, Elisa; childhood and youth, 13, 16, 28, 31, 34; marriage, 40–1, 43; Imperial Highness, 59; and Napoleon's divorce, 95; and Madame Mère, 112, 114; Napoleon's provision for, 120; at Trieste, 143; death, 160–1, 164
Bacchioci, Felix, 40–1, 43
Bacher, Dr., 67
Baden, Grand Duke of, 75
Balzac, Honoré de, 113

Barras, Paul, Vicomte de, 36
Bastia, 3, 13, 15, 16, 26, 134
Bastille, fall of, 24
Bathurst, Henry, 3rd Earl, 144, 147–50
Battersby, Captain, 125–6
Bausset, de, 117n
Beauharnais, Eugène de, 47, 66, 75, 94, 117n, 120, 151, 165, 168
Beauharnais, Hortense de, Queen of Holland; and Josephine, 47, 94; marriage to Louis, 52; children, 67, 75, 175–6; separation from Louis, 87, 100–1, 103, 110, 146; and Napoleon, 100, 118, 135–6, 165; relations with Madame Mère, 139–41, 175–6, 178, 182
Beauharnais, Josephine de (*see* Josephine, Empress)
Beauharnais, Stéphanie de, 75
Beaumont, General de la Bonninière de, 66
Belette, the, 31,
Bellerophon, the, 147,
Bennigsen, General, 114
Bernadotte, Madame, 47
Bernadotte, Marshal, 43, 47, 50–1, 51n, 114
Berthier, Marshal, 42
Bertrand, Fanny, Comtesse, 136–7, 184
Bertrand, Henri, General Comte, 124–5, 128, 145, 160, 164
Beugnot, Comte, 92
Beurnonville, General, 92–3

Billon, 34
Blachier, Madame, 125
Blessington, Lady, 153-4
Blessington, Lord, 154
Blou, Madame de, 125
Blücher, General, 114, 117, 136
Bocognano, 30
Bonaparte, Alexandrine (2nd wife of Lucien), 53-6, 61-2, 64-5, 90-1, 96-8, 139, 170
Bonaparte, Carlo, 1-8, 12-13, 15-18, 22, 24, 26, 60, 186
Bonaparte, Caroline (*see* Murat)
Bonaparte, Catherine, Queen of Westphalia (second wife of Jerome), 63n, 84-5 94, 100, 106, 113-15, 118-19, 150, 154, 157, 165
Bonaparte, Charles-Lucien (son of Lucien), 169
Bonaparte, Charlotte ('Lolotte', daughter of Lucien), 54, 90-1, 95-7, 99, 166, 178-80
Bonaparte, Charlotte (daughter of Joseph), 169, 176-7
Bonaparte, Christine (first wife of Lucien), 34, 53
Bonaparte, Elisa (*see* Bacchiochi)
Bonaparte, Jerome, King of Westphalia; childhood and education, 7, 17, 22, 29, 31, 33; character, 62, 80, 87-8; early career, 41, 45, 49, 62-3; marriage to Miss Patterson, 62-3, 66, 84; marriage to Catherine of Würtemberg, 63n, 84-5, 113, 115; King of Westphalia, 84, 86; and Madame Mère, 94, 106, 134-5, 146, 154, 160, 174, 176-8, 185; and fall and death of Napoleon, 119-20, 143, 151, 165-6, 183; tomb in the Invalides, 186
Bonaparte, Joseph, King of Spain; childhood and education, 4, 6, 9-10, 12-13, 16-17, 22-3; as head of the family, 19, 21, 23, 39, 54, 187; character, 21-3; career, 26-7, 33, 36, 43, 44, 46-7, 49, 74, 78, 118-19; marriage, 34; and Madame Mère, 50, 57, 86, 135; and the succession to Napoleon, 54-6, 59; mediates between Napoleon and Lucien, 54, 65; King of Spain, 90, 108, 115-16; Napoleon's provision for, 120; in U.S.A., 142-3, 149-51, 160, 177; and death of Napoleon, 165, 183; tomb in the Invalides, 186
Bonaparte, Jules-Laurent-Lucien (son of Lucien), 53-4
Bonaparte, Julie, Queen of Spain, 34-5, 110, 119, 134, 139, 165, 170-1, 173, 177-8
Bonaparte, Letizia (Madame Mère); birth, 1n; marriage, 1-4; appearance, 2n, 8, 15, 19, 42, 49, 68-9, 84, 93, 135, 153-4, 171; character, 2-3, 6-7, 10, 34, 38, 69, 89, 93, 106, 129, 171, 175, 187-8; birth of her children, 4-5, 7; attitude to money, 9, 12-13, 19, 21-3, 32, 38, 50, 58, 67, 75-9, 82, 86, 88-9, 92-3, 102, 124, 146-7, 150-1; and Corsican politics, 25-31, 43-6; takes refuge in France, 30-3; and death of Duc d'Enghien, 56-7; in Rome, 58-61, 123-4, 139, 143-85; *Souvenirs of*, 88, 131, 163-4; schemes for 'Lolotte', 90-1, 95-7, 99; desire for title and position, 59-62, 66-7, 74-9; at the château of Pont, 71-5, 79, 83, 110-11, 113-14, 116, 124, 127; on Elba, 124-31, 134, 184; believes Napoleon has left St. Helena, 159-61; and Napoleon's last illness and death 156-8, 161-6; her illness, 168, 170, 172, 178, 185; death and burial, 185; (*see also under* Bacchiochi, Elisa; Beauharnais, Hortense de; Bonaparte, Jerome, Joseph, Louis and Lucien; Borghese, Princess Pauline; Fesch, Cardinal; Josephine, Empress; Marie-Louise, Empress; Napoleon I)

Index

Bonaparte, Letizia (daughter of Lucien), 61
Bonaparte, Louis, King of Holland; childhood and education, 7–8, 13, 22–3, 26; career, 33–4, 36, 45–7, 49; marriage to Hortense, and separation, 52, 87, 95, 100–1, 103; and Napoleon, 54–6, 59, 100–5, 115–16; King of Holland, and abdication, 74, 101–3, 108, 110, 112, 116; character, 84, 101, 103; and Madame Mère, 23–4, 100–6, 110–13, 116, 124, 143, 146, 165; troubles with Fesch, 170, 183
Bonaparte, Louis-Napoleon (see Napoleon III)
Bonaparte, Lucien, Prince of Canino; childhood and education, 7, 13, 16–17, 23; relations with Napoleon, 21, 50–9, 63–6, 79–81, 86–7, 95–8, 135, 137; character, 28, 35, 47, 51; as Corsican politician, 28–9, 30n, 33; relations with Madame Mère, 34, 44, 51, 54–6, 58–9, 58–9, 61–6, 79–81, 86–7, 90–1, 95–9, 104, 107, 110, 124, 127, 132–3, 146, 170, 177, 185; career, 35–6, 46–51, 53; first marriage, 34, 53; second marriage, 54–6, 61–2, 64–5; Prince of Canino, 90, 139; captured by British, 104, 108; and Napoleon's death, 162, 165–6
Bonaparte, Maria-Anna, 7, 9
Bonaparte, Princess Mathilde, 12, 156
Bonaparte, Napoleon-Louis (son of Louis), 166, 169, 175–7
Bonaparte, Paul-Marie (son of Lucien), 169
Bonaparte, Pauline (see Borghese, Princess Pauline)
Bonaparte, Prince Victor (grandson of Jerome), 44n
Bonaparte, Zénaïde (daughter of Joseph), 44n, 169
Borghese, Prince Camillo, 53, 147

Borghese, Princess Pauline; childhood and girlhood, 7, 22, 29–31, 33–4, 39; illness of, 39, 110, 160; marriage to General Leclerc, 42–4, 47, 53; marriage to Prince Camillo Borghese, 53, 147; and Madame Mère, 48–50, 58, 92–3, 95, 97, 102, 106, 110, 143, 147n; during the Empire, 74, 94, 100; Napoleon's provision for, 120, 165; on Elba, 129, 131–3, 137–8; and Napoleon's exile on St. Helena, 157–62; and Napoleon's death, 165, 168; death of, 168–9
Bou, Mademoiselle, 20
Boulanger, Madame Clément, 154–5
Boulogne, Abbé, 73
Bourbonne-les-Bains, 15
Bourdier, Dr., 67
Bourrienne, Fauvelet, de, 37n, 46n
Bressieux, Madame de, 66, 69
Brienne, military college at, 14–17
Buonaparte, Francisco, 2
Buonavita, Abbé, 125, 157, 161–3, 165
Byron, Lord, 120n, 133n, 144, 153
Byron, Lady, 120n

Cadoudel, Georges, 56
Calvi, 3–4, 31
Cambacérès, Jean-Jacques, Arch-Chancellor, 93–4, 113, 116
Camerata, Countess (daughter of Elisa), 176–8
Campbell, Colonel Neil, 125–6, 130, 132–3
Campi, 64 and n, 95–8
Canova, Antonio, 88, 151, 168
Capitello tower, 30, 81
Carlos IV, King of Spain, 53–4
Caroline, the
Casabianca, M. de, 70
Casanova, General Arrighi de, Duke of Padua, 183–5

Castiglione, Benedetto di, 82
Castlereagh, Robert Stewart, Viscount, 144, 149, 164
Caterina (servant to Madame Mère), 7, 23
Chaptal, Jean, 62
Chardon, Abbé, 14
Charles IX, King of France, 187
Charles X, King of France, 57, 171
Charles V, the Emperor, 99
Charles, Captain, 42, 45
Chateaubriand, François Réné de, 9, 53, 141, 153, 173 and n
Cholet, M. de, 70
Clary, Desirée, 47
Clary, Julie (*see* Bonaparte, Julie, Queen of Spain)
Clary, Madame, 44
Cochelet, Mademoiselle, 135
Cochrane, Lord, 169
Colchen, J. V., 8n
Coll'Alto, Counts of, 2
Colonna, Simeon, 125, 140, 152, 159, 161, 182
Concordat of 1801, 51–2
Consalvi, Cardinal, 143, 156n, 165
Corbière, Comte de, 142
Corneille, 24, 131, 188
Corsica, and England, 3–5, 28; history of, 2–6, 25–31, 41, 43, 117
Corte, 2–4
Corvisart, Dr., 67, 72
Cossé-Brissac, Duc de, 66, 69–70
Cossé-Brissac, Duchesse de, 70
Costa, 29–30
Coti, Abbé, 29
Coursot, 157, 165

Dambré, Edouard, 182
Davout, Madame, 66
Decazes, Elie, 110, 140
Désormaux, Dr., 67
Diderot, Denis, 39
Doria, Monseigneur, 25
Dryade, the, 134

Du Cayla, Madame, 139n
Dumas, Alexandre, 174

Egyptian campaign, 45, 47
Elba, 124–30, 134–6, 147, 157, 184
Elliot, Sir Gilbert, 43n
Enghien, Louis-Antoine, Duc d', 56–7, 57n, 70
Eugénie, Empress, 44n
Eylau, battle of, 81, 83

Ferdinand I, King of the Two Sicilies, 167
Ferdinand III of Tuscany, 141
Fesch, Cardinal Joseph; education, 13; and death of Carlo, 17; and his nephews, 22, 66, 80, 108–9, 126, 170, 183; flight to France, 29, 31; and Madame Mère, 45, 49, 58–60, 82, 95, 97, 108–10, 112–13, 123, 134, 138–45, 155–7, 159, 166, 170, 176, 182–3; character, 45; Cardinal, 52–3, 67; during Napoleon's exile on St. Helena, 146, 151, 159–61; and Napoleon's death, 163, 165
Fesch, Grandmother, 6, 11, 23, 29
Flahaut, General de, 87
Fleurieu, Madame de, 66, 69
Fontanes, Louis de, 101n
Fontanges, Baronne de, 66, 69, 89–90
Fouché, Joseph, 50, 57
Francis I, Emperor of Austria, 40, 96, 105, 107, 113–14, 119–20, 158
Frederick the Great, 85n
Frederick William III of Prussia, 158
Fréjus, 47
Fréron, Stanislas, 39
Friedland, battle of, 81, 84

Gabrielli, Princess (daughter of Lucien), 54, 90–1, 95–7, 99, 166, 178–80
Gaffori, 25
Genoa, 2–4, 41
George III, 164
Gérard, painter, 58, 151

Giubega, Laurent, 9, 31
Gobert, actor, 174
Goethe, 169
Golfe-Juan, 133–4
Grasshopper, the, 125
Gregory VII, Pope, 175–6, 186
Gros, Jean-Antoine, 151
Guieu, Baron, 75–9, 110

Helfert, J. A. von, 129n
Henri III, King of France, 187
Héreau, Dr., 67
Hesse-Homburg, Prince of, 123
Hobhouse, John Cam, 144
Holland, Lord, 148–9, 162
Honorati, Princess Jeanne (Lucien's daughter), 169
Hood, Admiral, 28, 32
Howard, Lord, 149n
Huboy, O., 148n

Ilari, Camillia, 7
Isabey, J-B, 151
Isoard, Monseigneur d', 58n

Joaquim, the, 134
Josephine, Empress, marriage to Napoleon, 36–8, 47, 49; character and way of life, 38–9, 42, 45–6, 54n; and Madame Mère, 37–8, 41–2, 45, 48–50, 52, 67, 83, 94–5; and the death of the Duc d'Enghien, 56–7; as Empress, 59, 66–8, 82–5; divorced from Napoleon, 46, 85, 94–5, 101, 120, 136
Jouberthon, Madame de, 53–4 (*see also* Bonaparte, Alexandrine)
Julius Caesar, 132, 137
Junot, General (*later* Duc d'Abrantès), 34, 42, 48n, 168
Justinian, 24

Koller, General, 129n

Labord-Mériville, Madame de, 66
La Bouillerie, Baron de, 119

Lannes, Marshal, 42
Laplace, Pierre-Simon, Marquis de, 19
Lariboisière, Ferdinand de, 92n
Larrey, Baron, 19, 166n, 176n
Las Cases, Emmanuel, Comte de, 145–6, 151, 157, 159–60, 188
Launay, Mademoiselle de, 67
Leclerc, General, 42–4, 47, 53
Leclerc, Pauline (*see* Borghese, Princess Pauline)
Leghorn, 125–6
Leipzig, battle of, 114–15
Leoben, battle of, 40
Liverpool, Robert, 2nd Earl of, 144, 161–2
Loménie de Brienne, Madame, 72n
Longwood House, 145, 147, 183, 188
Loti, Pierre, 155n
Louis XIII, 73, 187
Louis XIV, 67, 71, 85, 99
Louis XV, 3, 5–6, 71
Louis XVI, 24, 26, 28, 66
Louis XVIII, 124, 130, 139–40, 143, 165
Louis-Philippe, 171–3, 173n
Lowe, Sir Hudson, 43, 144–50, 174
Lucan, Lord, 149
Lucien, Archdeacon, 2, 5–6, 9–10, 12, 21, 26

Macchiavelli, 24
Machielli, Dr., 156
Madrid, 51, 53, 64n
Maintenon, Madame de, 16, 160
Malet, General, 111
Malmaison, 45, 49, 136, 175
Marbeuf, Comte de, 6, 8–9, 13
Marchand, Louis, 126, 132, 134–5, 137n, 148n, 164–5
Marengo, battle of, 141, 183
Maret, Hugues, Duc de Bassano, 94
Maria-Federovna, Empress of Russia, 187
Marie-Amélie, Queen, 139

Marie-Antoinette, Queen, 15, 45, 99
Marie de Medicis, Queen, 49
Marie-Louise, Empress, 96, 99–100, 102, 107, 109–13, 116, 118–22, 141, 154, 163, 176, 180–2, 187; and Madame Mère, 100, 107, 110–11, 120–1, 154, 163, 180–2
Marie-Louise, Queen of Etruria, 54
Marmont, Marshal, 34
Marseilles, 32–3, 35–9, 41, 81
Masson, F., 102–3, 105, 109, 144
Matthew, General, 149
Mazuyer, Valérie, 175, 176n
Mellini, Rosa, 128, 152, 155, 161, 178, 182
Méry, Joseph, 170–1
Metternich, Prince, 39, 45, 114, 140, 178
Milan, 39–42, 44, 64, 68, 86
Mirabeau, Victor, Marquis de, 26
Moncey, Marshal, 119
Monge, Dr., 8–9
Montaigne, 21
Montesquieu, 21
Montfort, Prince and Princess de, 153–4
Montholon, Charles, Comte de, 15, 164
Moore, Thomas, 133n
Moreau, General, 56
Murat, Caroline, Queen of Naples; childhood and girlhood, 7, 15, 22, 31, 33–4, 41; marriage to Murat, 49, 52; during the Empire, 59, 75, 94, 100; and Napoleon, 117, 165; and death of Madame Mère, 170, 183
Murat, Joachim, King of Naples, 42, 45, 49, 52, 74, 94, 111, 117, 146

Napoleon I; childhood and education, 6, 9–18, 67, 179; relations with Madame Mère, 11–18, 21–4, 27, 31, 37–40, 44–7, 50, 54–63, 66–8, 71–85, 88–9, 107, 115, 126–9, 134–60, 187–8; military career, 4, 19–20, 23–4, 27, 32–43, 45–6, 109–12, 114, 117–19; *Essay on Suicide*, 20; *Letters from Corsica*, 25; and Corsican politics, 24–31; and Josephine, 36–8, 46–7, 49, 85, 94–5; First Consul, 48–9, 50–2; Emperor, 37n, 54, 59–61, 67, 73; attempts to assassinate, 48–9, 51, 93; and the death of the Duc d'Enghien, 56–7; and the Tsar, 81, 88, 90, 109; marriage to Marie-Louise, 96, 99–100; abdication, 120; on Elba, 125–31, 135–6, 184; the Hundred Days, 131–8; on St. Helena, 143–51, 154, 156–63, 171, 173; illness and death, 161–5, 186; (*see also under* Bonaparte, Jerome, Joseph, Louis and Lucien)
Napoleon II (*see* Rome, King of)
Napoleon III, 44n, 142, 171–2, 175–6, 186
Nasica, Judge, 27
Nelson, Horatio, Lord, 43n
Nice, 32–4

O'Meara, Dr., 156
Orléans, Duc d' (*later* Louis-Philippe), 171–3
Orléans, Duchesse d' (*later* Queen Marie-Amélie), 139
Orsay, Comte d', 153

Padua, General Arrighi de Casanova, Duke of, 183–5
Paoli, Giacinto, 3
Paoli, Pasquale, 3–5, 20, 24–31, 188
Paravicini, Gertrude, 9
Patterson, Elizabeth, 62–3, 63n
Permon, Laure (*see* Abrantès, Duchesse d')
Permon, Madame, 48 and n
Pibru, Dufaur, 122
Pichegru, Charles, 56
Pietra-Santa, Angela-Maria, 2
Pietri, François, 53n
Planat de la Faye, Louis, 159n
Pius VII, Pope, 58–9, 61, 67, 90, 92, 108–9, 112–13, 123–4, 139, 143–4,

156; with Madame Mère in Rome, 144, 152, 165, 170, 175
Plato, 24
Plutarch, 14
Porto-Ferrajo, 125–6
Possé, Comtesse de (daughter of Lucien), 166
Potocka, Countess, 14n, 84
Pozzo di Borgo, Carlo Andrea, 7n, 43n
Pozzo di Borgo, Maria, 7
Pressigny, Monseigneur de, 143
Prokesch von Osten, 176–80

Racine, 24, 68, 118
Raguideau, notary, 37 and n
Ramolino, André, 44n
Ramolino family, 2
Recco, Abbé, 10
Regnault, painter, 85
Regnault de St. Jean d'Angély, Comte de, 94–5
Reichstadt, Duke of (*see* Rome, King of)
Ris, M. de, 70
Robaglia (secretary to Madame Mère), 182
Robespierre, Charlotte de, 34
Robespierre, Maximilien de, 34–5
Rochefort d'Ailly, Madame de, 66
Roëll, M., 101n
Rohan-Chabot, Princesse de, 57
Rome, 58–61, 123–4, 139, 143–85
Rome, King of, 10, 105–7, 111–13, 118–19, 165, 171, 175–6, 178–83, 186
Rosebery, Lord, 148
Rousseau, Jean-Jacques, 3, 21

Saint-Cyr, convent school of, 16, 28
St. Helena, 11, 18–19, 32, 52, 57, 82n, 85n, 105, 117, 125n, 128, 130, 132, 138, 141–51, 154–63, 171, 173, 180, 183–4
St. Maximin, 33, 35

Saint-Pern, Madame de, 66, 69
Saint-Sauveur, Madame de, 66
Saliceti, 33
Santa Cruz, Marquesa de, 53
Santini, Natale, 147–8
Sartrouville, Madame de, 152 and n, 155 and n, 161–2, 178
Saveria (servant to Madame Mère), 7, 67, 125–6, 152, 169
Schoenbrunn, 180
Schwarzenberg, Prince, 114
Skelton, Colonel, 145
Skelton, Mrs., 145–6
Soult, Madame, 66
Soult, Marshal, 115
Stabs, 93
Stendhal, 39, 143, 186–7
Strabi, Monseigneur, 169

Talleyrand-Périgord, Charles-Maurice de, 57, 65–6, 107–8
Talma, François-Joseph, tragedian, 138
Theodore I, King of Corsica, 3
Thorvaldsen, B., 185n
Tilsit, treaty of, 81, 84
Torlonia, banker, 149
Toulon, 31–3, 36, 39, 81, 122
Touvenin, Bernard, 182
Tower, Commander, 149
Tuscany, Ferdinand III of, 141

Valence, 19–20, 27, 69
Venice, 183
Vercelli, Bishop of, 66, 73
Versailles, 13, 15, 71–2
Vienna, taken by Napoleon, 91–2; Congress of, 130, 133
Vignali, Abbé, 157
Voltaire, 21

Wagram, battle of, 92, 183
Walewska, Countess Maria, 82–3
Waterloo, battle of, 9, 85n, 117, 136
Württemberg, King of, 63n, 84, 115, 143